The Seeds Of Achievement

The Ultimate Roadmap For Teens and Young Adults On How They Can Obtain Success, Prosperity, Life Harmony, Super Achiever Status and The Winning Edge In Life Years Before They Should Have

By Scott G. Nicholson

Become a Super Achiever NOW!

The Seeds Of Achievement

The Ultimate Roadmap For Teens and Young Adults On How They Can Obtain Success, Prosperity, Life Harmony, Super Achiever Status and The Winning Edge <u>In Life Years Before They Should Have</u>

ISBN–978–0–6151–8519–4

Published by
INNOVENTION MARKETING, LLC.
Bohemia, NY

First Printing

TABLE OF CONTENTS

INTRODUCTION

This will be the most important book you ever read in your life! No other information source will provide you with the critical and essential information you will need to attain success, prosperity, life harmony, Super Achiever status and the winning edge in life. Without this book in your life, your chances of obtaining all your heart's desires, dreams and goals will be significantly lower. Without this book in your life, you will never reach you true greatest potential. Without this book in your life, you will never capture the extreme levels of success and prosperity that you have the potential to obtain. WITH THIS BOOK IN YOUR LIFE, YOU WILL BE ABLE TO ACHIEVE ANYTHING YOUR HEART DESIRES!

Now that I hope to have captured your attention, let me say CONGRATULATIONS! By purchasing this book, you are obviously serious about attaining success and greatness in your life and have just taken the first, and most important step towards significantly increasing your chances of obtaining life success ten, twenty, maybe thirty years sooner than you would have had you never purchased this book! Is that exciting or what!

Imagine obtaining most of the knowledge, information, skills, personal traits and characteristics on how to possess and obtain success and prosperity that you would normally have at forty years old, in your twenties. Think about how much more successful and prosperous you would be if you could apply all this information to your life and career RIGHT NOW, rather than having to wait ten to twenty years to learn it all.

Possessing this information NOW will enable you to make better decisions in life, and handle personal, school and career situations far more efficiently, avoid life and career complications and obstacles, enhance career opportunities, improve your personal and family relationships, keep yourself organized and maintain mental and physical strength. Having this information NOW will truly impact your life in ways you could never imagine.

Just like the seeds of a tree that builds its foundations and provides the essential ingredients and nutrients necessary for it to grow, the information in this book will be the "SEEDS OF KNOWLEDGE" that will provide you with the essential ingredients and nutrients for you to grow, mature and succeed in your life. Remember, every redwood tree, the largest tree on earth, was once a seedling. You too can become a redwood tree with potential to reach unlimited success and prosperity. It starts with this book.

You are obviously a young individual who plans on obtaining great things in your life. This book will assist you in not only reaching, but surpassing all of your life and career goals by educating and training you on the most critical and important personal traits, characteristics and life-skills that will catapult you past all your competition and enable you to succeed in whatever it is you want to achieve and obtain.

When you complete this book, you will be part of an elite group of individuals that I call *SUPER ACHIEVERS!* SUPER ACHIEVERS are those individuals in society that are in the TOP 5% of all successful and prosperous individuals. What sets them apart from 95% of all others is the fact that they have succeeded in becoming incredibly successful in **ALL** areas of their lives, not just one or two. They are not only wealthy and financially independent, but they also have succeeded in obtaining harmony, prosperity and happiness in their family and personal lives and have the highest levels of self-confidence and self-esteem of the vast majority of people in society today. This balance of success across the three critical areas of your life, which we will discuss in more depth shortly, gives the SUPER ACHIEVERS the "THE WINNING EDGE" in life. This WINNING EDGE IN LIFE is what sets apart the SUPER ACHIEVERS FROM ALL OTHERS and is the deciding factor that will separate you from all other people you come in contact with throughout your life and career. Possessing the WINNING EDGE IN LIFE will be directly responsible for you winning more, achieving more, possessing more, experiencing **LUCK** more, meeting other successful individuals more and being filled with more happiness, wealth, organization, life-balance and prosperity. Possessing THE WINNING EDGE will provide you with the high levels of integrity, motivation, organization, confidence, physical and mental strength you will need to fear nothing in life and strive to attain all you wish to achieve. And, what's most exciting, you will obtain all these things ten, twenty, maybe thirty years sooner than you would have if you had never read this book. THIS IS MY PROMISE TO YOU!

Becoming a SUPER ACHIEVER, obtaining the WINNING EDGE OF LIFE and possessing the rare, yet exhilarating balance of success across the three most important areas of your life is what this book strives to teach you how to obtain.

The information obtained in THE SEEDS OF ACHIEVEMENT is a wealth of information that most average individuals would partially learn over the course of their lives through their life's experiences, reading and their natural maturing and educational process. This natural type of learning takes years to naturally develop. By the time they finally learn all the aspects, traits, characteristics and tactics of how to become successful and achieve SUPER ACHIEVER STATUS with THE WINNINGE EDGE OF LIFE, they are in the middle of their lives. WHY WAIT UNTIL THEN TO BECOME A SUPER ACHIEVER? WHY WAIT UNTIL YOU'RE FORTY OR FIFTY TO OBTAIN THE WINNING EDGE OF LIFE? WHY WAIT TO POSSESS SOME OF THE MOST POWERFUL AND EFFECTIVE TRAITS TO ASSIST YOU IN OBTAINING GREATNESS? WHY CAN'T YOU OBTAIN ALL THESE THINGS IN YOUR YOUTH? At twenty-two, twenty, maybe even eighteen or sixteen. Now you can through the teachings in this book!

The SEEDS OF ACHIEVEMENT will fast forward your learning curve and educate you on what it takes to become successful YEARS SOONER THAN THE AVERAGE INDIVIDUAL. By learning and possessing this information earlier in life, you will increase your chances of achieving your heart's desires at a much earlier age, which in turn will enable you to reap the benefits and rewards of greatness while you still possess your youth! NOW THAT IS EXCITING! Now, let's begin gardening and plant some seeds!

CHAPTER #1

What Is True Success

CHAPTER 1: What Is True Success?

Unfortunately, in today's society, success is measured by wealth, social status, fame and material possessions. While these four things do usually go hand in hand with success, TRUE SUCCESS in life means so much more.

You probably have seen numerous news stories about the rich and famous who possess lives of great luxury and financial wealth. Movie stars, politicians, music stars, chief executives, they all seem to be hugely successful on the surface. However, in many cases, the only successful parts of their lives are their careers, which provides the wealth and fame. In many cases, they are anything but successful in their personal and individual lives. While they are consumed in financial and material abundance, their personal and individual lives are in complete disarray due to the unethical and immoral way they lead their lives and the people that they associate with. Drug use, alcohol abuse, immorality, and low ethical standards cause many of these individuals to live in a world filled with personal problems, health problems, and relationship problems. All the fame, money and material possessions in the world never make up for this type of lifestyle. Do you call this success? I sure don't.

True success is so much more than wealth, fame, career success or material possessions. True success in life is possessing an EQUAL BALANCE of success across three of the most essential areas of our life. I call this the CRITICAL 3s.

1)   Your Personal Success
2)   Your Career Success
3)   Your Individual Success (Self)

Without possessing success in all three of these areas of your life, you will never experience the exhilarating feeling of obtaining true success and prosperity in your life.

Before you can even begin to take steps to achieve true success, you must first PREPARE YOURSELF AND YOUR MIND FOR SUCCESS. What do I mean? Well, in order to ensure that you have WHAT IT TAKES, to begin your journey towards true success, you must be sure you take five critical success preparation steps which will ensure that you not only stay on your success path until all your goals are achieved, but will also ensure that the actions and decisions you make along your journey are the right, and most productive ones to take.

The first, and most important step you must take is the REPROGRAMMING OF YOUR MIND to have a clear focus on EXACTLY WHAT YOU WANT TO ACHIEVE. Condition your mind for success! You must know, without a shadow of a doubt, what you want to achieve, be or do. Without this reprogramming in place, you will never have the stamina, drive or conviction to do what it takes to achieve your goal.

The second step is KNOWING THE OUTCOME. You must visualize and believe what the final outcome WILL BE. You must see yourself achieving or doing whatever your heart's desire is. Remember, **SEEING IS BELIEVING**. What your mind thinks it is.....It is!

The third step is COMMITTING TO TAKE ACTION NOW! You must commit to take immediate action towards your goals. Make the first call, send the letter, meet the decision maker, send the resume and ask for a meeting. Whatever steps you need to take to achieve your goal, you must take them now. You must demand more from yourself than anyone else would. You must move faster, and more effectively than any other individual YOU KNOW in order to get the prize. That prize being unlimited success and prosperity in your world.

Commit to get better and closer to your goals EVERY DAY through small advancements. Just like in weightlifting, when you begin with lighter weights and daily and gradually increase the weight as your strength and muscle tone increases, so will your progress toward your goals. Don't try and conquer the world, or your goals, in a day. It won't happen. Commitment to consistent advancements and progress on a daily and weekly basis is the answer to you attaining greatness.

The fourth step is TAKING NOTICE OF YOUR RESULTS. The worst thing you can do is to commit to consistent progress, spend all your time and effort trying to attain your goals and get no results. This becomes counter productive and wastes your valuable time that you could be spending doing productive things. Every few weeks, ask yourself, "Are the actions I am taking getting me closer to achieving my goals?" If the answeris NO.......STOP! Make a change. Either change the things you are doing to achieve your goal or simply change your goal immediately into another area, field, or goal you so desire. Don't let poor results derail your inertia. You must find that special goal or desire in your life that you will have a passion for and tailor your efforts around TAKING productive steps towards your goal THAT SHOW RESULTS.

Remember, failure and poor results from your past or present mean nothing to your future! It is never too late to MAKE THAT CRITICAL CHANGE towards results oriented goal advancements.

Once your REPROGRAMMING has been achieved, the next important area of success that you need to understand is that in order to attain true greatness and Super Achiever status, you absolutely must possess a successful balance of the three essential areas of your life. This balance is what I call the SEESAW PRINCIPLE.

The See –Saw Principle

The SEE-SAW PRINCIPLE in one of the most powerful lessons for you to learn, understand and strive to attain. It is total symmetry and balance of the CRITICAL 3s. It is striving to achieve equal success and prosperity, not JUST in your career, not JUST in your personal life and not JUST in your individuality, but in all three at once. View the diagram below (Fig #1). As you can see, when you attain success in the CRITICAL 3s, your life is filled with BALANCE, ORGANIZATION, MOTIVATION, SELF-CONFIDENCE, STABILITY, HAPPINESS, SELF- ESTEEM AND OVERALL LIFE PROSPERITY. Without equal balance and success in your career and personal life, the SEE-SAW becomes unbalanced causing an area of your life to become unstable, problematic or negative. Without success with your SELF, or INDIVIDUALITY, how you feel about yourself as a person, the whole support structure (FULCRUM), becomes unstable, negatively affecting both your personal life and your career. The SEE-SAW principle is a simplistic, easy to understand example of the importance of striving and attaining success across all the key areas of your life. Without symmetry and balance OF SUCCESS in the CRITICAL 3'S, you will never reach your true potential in life.

Fig #1.

Personal Life		Career

Self

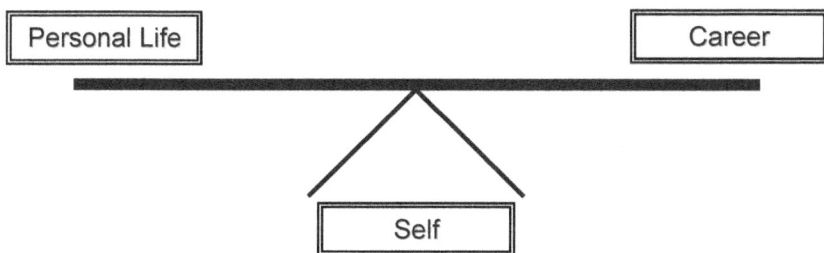

Every word and every chapter of this book is focused on steering you towards learning, understanding and finally implementing all of the traits, tactics and characteristics you will need to ensure that you attain complete balance with your success!

The Winning Edge of Life / Super Achievers

I briefly touched on the great importance of possessing THE WINNING EDGE OF LIFE and how possessing this will enable you to become a SUPER ACHIEVER. However, I want to ensure that you truly understand what THE WINNING EDGE OF LIFE really is.

My official definition of THE WINNINGE EDGE OF LIFE is...That which gives an individual the slight margin of superiority and advantage over all others. Simplified, it's possessing the edge over your competition & life challenges.

Individual who possess the WINNINGE EDGE OF LIFE are not necessarily better or smarter than the average person, they simply develop and focus all their energies, talents and abilities in the specific areas of their lives and careers that make a significant difference in their performance and how they handle challenges in their lives. This gives them the decided advantage over the average person in their field or area of specialty. This does not just apply to careers. You can possess the WINNING EDGE OF LIFE in your personal life, and individual life as well.

Studies have shown that THE WINNING EDGE is usually a small difference in knowledge or talent that translates into ENORMOUS DIFFERENCES IN RESULTS. THESE ARE THE SUPER ACHIEVERS!

Two examples of how the WINNING EDGE makes a difference are as follows.

1) A major league baseball player with a batting average of .250 gets three hits per every twelve times at bat. In 1999, the average salary for a .250 hitter was $750,000.

   A major league baseball player with a batting average of .300, gets four hits every twelve times at bat, just one more hit, than the .250 hitter (small difference). In 1999, the average salary of a .300 hitter was $3,000,000. That's a 400% increase in salary for only one more additional hit in twelve at bats. (Enormous difference in results).

2) In horse racing, many outcomes are decided by a nose at the finish line (small difference). Now, one would think that the difference in earnings between the winning horse and the second place horse would not be too far apart right? Think again. The average purse for second place finishes in 1999 was $75,000. The average purse for the first place finisher was $1,250,000! Enormous difference in results winning by a nose. THAT'S THE WINNING EDGE OF LIFE. YOU NEED TO POSSESS IT!

One other example of why it is so important to strive to be a SUPER ACHIEVER and obtain THE WINNING EDGE OF LIFE is to review the conclusions of numerous studies attempting to find out what it takes to be successful and how rare being truly successful in life really is.

Studies have shown that on average, out of 100 people.....

1) Only 1 will be wealthy, prosperous and live in complete harmony in their personal and individual lives.

2) 80 will depend on pensions, still be working or broke by age 65.

3) 55 will be divorced.

4) 47 will have been fired or laid off from their jobs.

5) 60 will have some health problem.

6) 37 will seek psychiatric help.

By looking at these statistics, you would think that the chance of obtaining SUPER ACHIEVER STATUS and THE WINNING EDGE would be impossible. Not if you start striving for this at a young age.

The secret to obtaining THE WINNING EDGE OF LIFE is to, as early in your life as possible, identify and then focus on the specific winning edges you need in your life to become a SUPER ACHIEVER. Once you have identified what specific winning edge you need, you must concentrate on developing those winning edges so you can become superior in that area. It may be any goal, career or desire you have. If it's sports, you will want to dedicate yourself to improving your physical skills in that sport. If it's a career in medicine, law or teaching, you must identify what edges you need to be the best of the best and work at becoming the best of the best. Whatever you goal, dream or aspiration, look for the Winning Edge, capture it, learn it, improve at it and apply it. If you do this, nothing will stop you from achieving SUPER ACHIEVER status in it.

If you begin to take the steps now and educate yourself on what it takes to achieve a balanced life of success, you will be the one individual out of one hundred that experiences a life of greatness in all areas that you desire. Believe me, IT'S WORTH THE EFFORT. Keep on reading!

CHAPTER #2

The Seeds of Achievement

CHAPTER 2: The Seeds of Achievement

In my introduction, I discussed briefly how the SEEDS OF ACHIEVEMENT will fast forward your learning curve and educate you on what it takes to become successful YEARS SOONER THAN THE AVERAGE INDIVIDUAL. I explained that just like the seeds of a tree build its foundation and provide the essential ingredients and nutrients necessary for it to grow, this book will be the "SEEDS OF KNOWLEDGE" that will provide you with the essential ingredients and nutrients for you to grow, mature and succeed in your life.

I would like to spend a little time educating you on what actually makes up the "SEEDS" of achievement. Just like planting a tree, it requires a collection or handful of seeds for the tree to fully possess all of the natural elements it needs to thrive and grow. The same holds true for you. In order to achieve the Winning Edge and Super Achiever status, you will need to possess a collection of seeds in order for you to thrive and grow.

Officially, the seeds of achievement are those traits, tactics and skills necessary for an individual to increase the percentages of obtaining success, prosperity, happiness and financial security in one's career, personal life and individuality. These seeds are broken into two primary categories:

1) TRAITS OF ACHIEVEMENT
2) TACTICS OF ACHIEVEMENT

The effective use, combination and implementation of both the Traits of Achievement and the Tactics of Achievement TOGETHER, will significantly increase your changes of achieving Super Achiever Status and possessing the Winning Edge of Life.

TRAITS OF ACHIEVEMENT

The Traits of Achievement consist of thirty essential personality traits, which we will go into detail on in the next section, that YOU MUST LEARN, UNDERSTAND AND IMPLEMENT immediately into your life. Making these thirty-four traits part of your every day life is a great challenge and will require you to be focused and disciplined on each of them to make them become part of your being! Some traits may take longer than others to implement into your lives. The key is take one trait at a time, understand it, practice it and implement it into the CRITICAL 3'S of your life as quickly as possible. For each Trait of Achievement that you master and implement into your world, you will increase the percentages of you attaining Super Achiever status by approximately 3%. Just think, the faster you master the traits, the faster you attain your heart's desires and goals! Seems worth learning to me!

Let's now learn the seeds!

The Traits of Achievement

1) INTEGRITY

    a. Possessing high levels of Integrity in life is one of the single most important traits that you can possess. Whether it's in business life, family life or personal life, expressing and conducting yourself with integrity will be responsible for more success and happiness in your life than any other trait.

    Integrity is having the ability to choose right from wrong, ethics over convenience and truth over popularity. It's possessing the ability to ALWAYS DO THE RIGHT, MORAL AND ETHICAL thing in every area of your life.

    Possessing integrity is having moral soundness, being honest, and being free from corruptive influence or motive. It is what you as an individual choose to do, say and think each day of your life and how you conduct and convey yourself to others. Throughout your personal and career life, you will continually encounter people, situations, events and circumstances that will test your level of integrity. Circumstances dealing with money, success, fame, career advancement, relationships and morality will constantly surround you as you mature. In many cases, you will be torn between the external, monetary or physical rewards that can be associated with many different circumstances and using your integrity. I can tell you now that having the strength to utilize your integrity and ALWAYS DO OR SAY THE RIGHT, ETHICAL AND MORAL thing will always be the right decision. Many more times than not, when an individual puts their integrity on the back burner, and is influenced in a negative way to conduct themselves incorrectly, immorally or unethically, they experience nothing but failure, shame, disappointment and sadness.

I say to you now, live and breathe with the highest levels of integrity every day of your life. Always do what is right, moral, ethical and sound. If you do, you will reap rewards, success and happiness far greater than you ever imagined.

2) PASSION

a. In every area of your life, you must possess PASSION! Passion in life is boundless enthusiasm and desire to succeed. You must have a passion for your family, passion for your career, passion for success, passion to be the best you can be in every area of your life and career. Whether it's a passion to be the best father you can be, the greatest athlete or the finest doctor, attorney or business professional. Possessing an extreme level of passion in all you do will be directly responsible for you achieving your heart's desires.

All Super Achievers I know possess some of the highest levels of passion in existence. They know that if they do not have passion, they will never be motivated enough to persist at anything long enough to become the best of the best. And, until they become the best of the best at what they are doing, they will never reach their greatest potential.

Passion provides you with the internal energy and drive to do whatever it takes to achieve your goals. Passion gives you the FAILURE IS NOT AN OPTION attitude that is a requirement for all Super Achievers.

If you have passion, you will love whatever it is you are doing or what you are striving for. This is critical since the fastest way to failure is TO DO WHAT YOU DON'T LIKE OR DON'T WANT TO DO. One thing I can assure you of right now. If you are not absolutely in love with what you are doing, or striving to achieve, you will never achieve it to its fullest potential.

There's a big difference between having a desire to succeed and accepting failure. Everyone, to some degree has a desire to win. Some individuals have stronger desires than others, but in general, all people possess it. It's human nature.

However, the question to ask yourself is, can I live with failure or mediocrity? If your answer is no, you no doubt have a level of passion. High levels of passion will prevent you from failing. It's essential, critical and required to succeed.

If you have passion in whatever it is you are striving for......Grow it stronger. If you don't have passion for what you are striving for, you have two options:

    i. Get it fast or
   ii. Stop what you're doing and FIND WHAT IT IS THAT WILL MAKE YOU PASSIONATE. It is the goal or desire that makes you passionate that you will ultimately reach Super Achiever status in.

3) Common Sense

Common sense is something that most individuals lack! They say that most average people have tremendous amounts of common sense simply because they have never used any of it yet.

Common sense is being able to make the correct decision, say the correct thing or take the correct action. Most average people, because they are lacking common sense, continually fail in doing all of these things because they never seem to learn from their lives' experiences and translate what they have learned towards the rest of their lives.

In most average individuals, common sense is usually developed as a long process of experiences that enable them to recognize a pattern of events when the events occur again. To put it simply, it is common sense to not touch the hot stove again after you already touched it and burned yourself. That is a simple explanation, but it gets the point across.

You must possess the ability to excel in learning from your experiences, deriving lessons from those experiences and applying what you learned to your future.

Super Achievers have this ability. They possess extremely high amounts of common sense in all areas of their lives because they are always conscious of making sure that they not only learn from every single experience in their career and personal lives, but more importantly, they apply what they learned from their experiences to their future experiences. By doing this, they avoid making the same mistakes, saying the wrong things or taking the wrong actions over and over again.

4) Persistence

a. Few traits will impact your life with such power as possessing high levels of Persistence. Persistence is the one trait that sets Super Achievers apart from all others. It's the ACT OF CONTINUING ON.....NEVER GIVING UP! It's pursuing a goal, a dream a need or a desire with such vengeance, regardless of the barriers or roadblocks that may be encountered.

You can ask any star athlete, successful business person or anyone who has excelled in their life and career what is was that allowed them to achieve their goals. All will say that THEY NEVER GAVE UP! They did whatever was needed to get done to achieve their goals. Years of practicing, studying or working at one thing was what gave them the winning edge to achieve their ultimate dreams and goals.

Persistence is known as the KEEP ON KEEPING ON ATTITUDE. The ability to continually strive to achieve.

A very low percentage of humans have the level of persistence required to truly achieve greatness, the winning edge and Super Achiever status. That's why they say...IT IS LONELY AT THE TOP! True success seems to be largely a matter of HANGING ON AFTER ALL OTHERS HAVE LET GO. So few people get to the top because so many people simply LET GO.

Super Achievers NEVER LET GO UNTIL THEY ACHIEVE. They laugh at failure. Failing to hold on, meet a goal or achieve a desire on the first, second or third try simply inspires them to hold on longer and stronger, work harder and become more committed to attaining whatever it is they desire. In essence, the more they fail, the stronger and more motivated they become to achieve. It's persistence that gives you the energy to fight through these failing times to KEEP ON KEEPING ON until you reach your goal.

It is important to know that Persistence overshadows even talent as the most valuable resource in shaping an individual's life. Without it, you could have all the talent in the world, but if you don't possess the persistence to accompany that talent through the challenges and failures that one will more than likely face, you will never reach the top.

There's a very appropriate saying that goes....THE RACE GOES ALWAYS NOT TO THE FASTEST, SWIFTEST, BIGGEST OR STRONGEST BUT TO THE ONE WHO KEEPS ON RUNNING AND RUNNING AND RUNNING!

5) Charisma

a. Charisma is a trait that so few people possess, yet it is so important in attaining success and prosperity.

Have you ever looked at an individual that JUST LOOKS SUCCESSFUL. They dress wonderful, have a strong, confident walk, well groomed, well spoken and in excellent physical shape? Everything about them reeks of success, confidence, strength and assurance. These are the aspects of charisma.

Many of the most successful people in all areas of life possess the highest levels of charisma. These Super Achievers have gotten to their place in life by presenting and expressing themselves with all of the charismatic traits that allows them to be recognized as truly successful. And, as we will discuss later, truly successful individuals who achieve Super Achiever status all associate together.

Charisma is personal magnetism and charm. It's possessing a strong personal aura and presence. It's a rare personal quality that causes people to gravitate to you in order to be associated with you due to your level of strength and confidence. This works not only in professional life but also in personal lives. I know many people that have modest careers yet as fathers and mothers, they express themselves to their children and family members with great charisma. Hence, their children and family members gravitate and look up to them.

Possessing charisma is being conscious of things like:
  i. The way you dress.
  ii. The way you shake hands.
  iii. The way you conduct eye contact.
  iv. The way you talk with respect.
  v. The way you walk. Posture.
  vi. The way you keep you body and physique.
  vii. Your energy and enthusiasm level.
  viii. The way you make a first impression.

Possessing charisma is something you should continually strive to improve. The more successful you continually become, the more you will be required to utilize your charismatic ways as you begin to associate with more and more Super Achievers.

With high levels of charisma, you will LOOK GREAT, FEEL GREAT, ACT GREAT and all the people you come in contact with will feel the same way about you!

6) Courage

As I stated in the persistence section, Super Achievers LAUGH AT FAILURE! Do you how know how they are able to laugh at something that normally ruins most average individuals? COURAGE!

Super Achievers make the decision early in their lives to place their dreams, goals and desires far above their fears. They develop a mindset that allows them to never be afraid of taking on any new task, challenge, responsibility, goal or desire. They dare to take the first steps down what may appear to be difficult paths.

Possessing high levels of courage is without question possessing the winning edge. It allows you to take on most of the things that the average person would not due to their fears. By eliminating all others due to their fears, a clear path is naturally created that leads you closer and closer to the ultimate prize of achieving your goals and dreams.

Courage is a state or quality of mind or spirit that enables you to face danger, fear, difficulties, and life challenges with confidence, fearlessness, firmness and bravery.

Think about all of the brave and courageous individuals throughout history that possessed extreme levels of courage to achieve their dreams.

  i. Sir Edmund Hillary: First to scale Mt. Everest.
 ii. Neil Armstrong: First man on the moon.
iii. Jackie Robinson: First black baseball player.
 iv. Ronald Reagan: Ended communism is Russia.

And the list goes on. Courage...Without it, you will never press on past your fears and challenges. And if you do not press on past your fears and challenges, you will never attain your ultimate goals and dreams in life. Remember, you will always miss 100% of the shots that you don't take!

7) **Self-Esteem**

Before you can feel good about a career, a relationship, a job or any life situation, you must feel good about one important thing before anything else.....You must feel good about YOU! Possessing self-esteem is feeling 100% confident in yourself as a person. You like how you look, dress, walk, talk, act, conduct yourself in public and live your life. Super Achievers like everything about themselves. Not in a conceited way, but in a confident way. Because of their high level of self-esteem, the express high levels of integrity and charisma which I discussed earlier.

Possessing self-esteem is having respect for yourself, having pride in yourself and in the things you do in life. You're proud to be you and therefore express high levels of confidence in how you conduct yourself and live your life.

Before you can begin to follow the path to Super Achiever status, you must be sure that you possess true self-esteem. If you do, there is nothing you cannot achieve.

8) **Self Confidence**

Self-confidence goes hand in hand with self esteem. Having superior levels of self-confidence means that you have 100% faith and trust in yourself as a person, your unique skills, abilities knowledge and personal life. When you possess Super Achiever levels of self-confidence, you have the powerful ability to be free of all self-doubt and fear of failure. You are self-inspired to chase any dream, goal or desire you have because you know you will achieve or attain it. Failure, in your mind is not an option. Success is the only option.

With high levels of self-confidence Super Achievers will gain strength, courage, and confidence by every experience in which they stop to look fear in the face.

Self-confident individuals also LOOK CONFIDENT. Their whole personal presence generates success, happiness, and harmony. You can instantly tell a Super Achiever apart from all other people,

The better you become, the smarter, wiser, and more knowledgeable you get, the more self-confident you become. Remember, you can never be too self-confident. Always strive to achieve and attain more and more self-confidence will naturally appear in you.

9) Character

Possessing high levels of character is critical in your quest for success and happiness in life. Character defines what you do, and who you are. Your level of character is revealed by the choices you make in your life, the promises you keep, and the level of trustworthiness you possess.

Possessing character is living your life with moral and ethical strength.

Super Achievers know that character is one of the few things that distinguishes them from all other individuals. Because so few people live lives based completely on the foundations of trust, keeping promises, morals and ethics, Super Achievers who possess this combined foundation of character traits naturally become some of the most admired, well respected, well liked and successful people in society. To be a Super Achiever, you must be all these things in whatever career or lifestyle path you take.

10)   Competence

Super Achievers understand that the future belongs to the most skilled, professional and knowledgeable people. Only those that are the best, and MOST COMPETANT in their area of specialty will reach the highest levels of success and happiness.

Possessing high levels of competence in all areas of your life is a key ingredient to obtaining true greatness in both your career and personal life. Having competence is being adequately or extremely well qualified in whatever field or area of life you require to be great in.

The only way to reach high levels of competence is to continue to work towards mastering that area of your life that you have chosen to set a path down. The more competent you become, the more you will continue to stand out as an individual in your chosen area.

The key is to work at becoming THE BEST IN YOUR FIELD OR AREA OF LIFE. You, like all Super Achievers, must live by the phrase JUST BEING GOOD IS NEVER ENOUGH. You have to become GREAT! So you are perceived as a high level, competent, individual.

The vast majority of individuals in business and life only desire to be associated with competent people. It is critical that you become just that in whatever it is you do.

11)   Creativity

When you look at an iceberg, as grand as it may be sticking high out of the water, your eyes only see 5% of the total size of the iceberg. Super Achievers look at the Iceberg and know that there is actually 95% more of the iceberg just below the surface. They have the ability to not only see the obvious, but also the vision to see what is not the obvious.

Thinking creatively is a trait that all Super Achievers possess. Where most individual's ideas are obvious and visible, Super Achievers look for that which is invisible to the average eye or mind. They think out of the box. They use this creative talent to set them apart from all others in their life. Much like the iceberg example above, Super Achievers know that what is easily seen by average eyes is only a small percentage of what is actually possible in life.

You must view all opportunities, ideas and your goals as if they are icebergs. Knowing that somewhere below the surface exists much more than the obvious.

12) <u>Positive Attitude</u>

There's an old expression that says, "Your attitude in life determines your altitude in life. No statement could be more true in the life of a Super Achiever.

Possessing a positive attitude in life is the positive mood that you approach all life situations with. A positive attitude is without question one of the most powerful traits an individual can possess. It causes a natural chain reaction of positive thoughts, events and outcomes that the non–positive thinker will never experience.

A positive attitude is a prerequisite for all Super Achievers. Everything they do or say is conducted in a positive, enthusiastic manner. Most Super Achievers are so positive, when they walk into the room of other people, everyone seems to become enlightened, positive, and enthusiastic simply in the Super Achiever's presence.

Even during tough times, Super Achievers have the unique ability to turn negativity, depression, sadness or difficulty into some positive form.

Super Achievers believe that their lives are not determined by what happens to them, but by the attitude they bring to life.

Because of this trait, Super Achievers are adored by others. People simply want to be around positive Super Achievers because the positive energy and attitude is contagious and others feed off it.

Be positive always and the world will be positive right back!

13) <u>Strive For Excellence</u>

Super Achievers strive for one thing and one thing only.....EXCELLENCE! In every aspect of their life, personal, relationships, friendships, career, health, communication etc, excellence is the one and only standard. There is no room for mediocrity in their minds.

Excellence is the result of the combination of Vision, Intention, Effort, Intelligence, Work Ethic, Passion, Dedication, Experience Practice and Skillful Execution. It's the constant flow of personal advancements, improvements and progress in the areas of your life you want to excel in. Your life mission should be to strive for excellence in all you do. Your constant quest for excellence will shape you and make you into the true WINNER you are soon to become.

Now, remember, becoming excellent and striving for excellence are two different things. It takes time, effort and extreme patience to become excellent in something. The key is to spend your life STRIVING TO ATTAIN EXCELLENCE in small, incremental stages of improvements over a period of time. Before you know it, the small incremental stages of improvements will begin to blend together, forming the building blocks of excellence you are looking for.

The more you strive, the more quickly you will become excellent at anything you desire. It's that simple!

14) Dedication, Desire and Passion

Possessing extreme levels of dedication, desire and passion are three of the most important personal traits any individual can have. In order to achieve unlimited success and prosperity, you must bind yourself intellectually, mentally, physically and emotionally to the course of action necessary to achieve your goals.

Super Achievers possess 100% dedication and passion towards their goals and dreams. They eat, breath, live and think about their success, how to achieve more success and attaining their goals EACH AND EVERY DAY! They have a burning desire to succeed at all times. They crave success! Failure is never an option. Even when failure does occur, they use the lessons of that failure to dedicate themselves to achieve something else, which is usually more dynamic.

Without question, the fastest way to failure is not possessing a passion for whatever it is you do. Passion is the driving force, the burning fire, and the eye of the tiger in your heart that provides you with the will, motivation, dedication, discipline and desire to take whatever steps necessary to achieve your goals.

The world's greatest achievers all had one thing very much in common. They all possessed a level of passion that far exceeded that of the average individual.

15) Enthusiasm

There is no more appealing trait an individual can possess than an enthusiastic, upbeat and positive personality. Those individuals who possess high levels of enthusiasm express lively expressions of joy and vigor, excitement and interest. Super Achievers always express enthusiasm for their life, career, company, family, future and personal life. This enthusiastic attitude has a powerful way of drawing only successful and positive people and circumstances directly to them. It's a very simple principle. Successful, enthusiastic, happy and joyful people are drawn to one another. They only enjoy being around other enthusiastic, happy, and joyful people. And, guess what happens when only successful, happy and joyful people all get together? They all become MORE successful, happy and joyful together.

Being enthusiastic will not only enhance your life, career and future. It will also create a magnetic draw to you of only the most successful and prosperous people in your chosen area of life. This is WHY Super Achievers live their life...ENTHUSIASTICALLY!

16) <u>Concentration and Focus</u>

At an airport, without the air traffic control tower focused on directing the hundreds of flights that are in its airspace, you can only imagine the disasters that could take place. Well, the same disasters can happen in your life without clear and precise concentration and focus on your goals and life plans.

With an average of 10,000 thoughts per day and over 3,000,000 thoughts per year, most individual's minds contain a collection of fragmented and cluttered thoughts and ideas that constantly flow in and out of one's brain. This constant flow of fragmented thoughts leads only to constant confusion, stress and failure as no task, idea, plan or goal is ever capable of being completed or attained. Being able to concentrate and focus on one task at a time, UNTIL COMPLETION, is a critical skill that you MUST possess in order to attain greatness and Super Achiever status in your life.

Super Achievers all possess the ability to direct all of their mental and physical energy in one direction to ensure the greatest and most effective outcome. In addition, they also focus all their time and attention to the completion of ONE THING, ONE TASK, ONE GOAL OR ONE IDEA at a time. They understand that what they focus and concentrate on THEY WILL BE AND BECOME.

Very simply, without extreme levels of focus and concentration on any one thing at a time, Goals will NEVER BE ATTAINED.

17) **Prioritization**

We now know the importance of focus and concentration. However, there is one trait that works in conjunction with focus and concentration that is essential to attaining success. That trait is Prioritization.

Prioritization is having the ability to focus and concentrate on one thing at a time BASED ON THE LEVEL OF IMPORTANCE. We all have important tasks, goals and responsibilities that need to get done each and every day. The key to accomplishing these is to take action on each task, goal or responsibility based on its level of importance or how, by not taking action on a specific task, it will negatively impact your life. You always want to take action on those tasks and responsibilities that will effect your day, week or life in the biggest way. Once you have taken action AND COMPLETED the highest priority tasks, move onto the second most important task, then the third and so on.

By taking life action steps based solely on priority, you will always be accomplishing the things in your life that will make the greatest, most positive impact.

18) **Humbleness**

In my professional opinion, one of the greatest traits for any individual to possess is humbleness. True Super Achievers are incredibly successful, but you would never know it by their actions, words or deeds. They are so extremely confident in themselves and their abilities that they do not need to express conceit or cockiness to others.

Most Super Achievers have attained their level of success through years of hard work, dedication, passion and desire. And because of this, they are grateful for their special gifts and talents and never boast, brag or degrade others.

On the flip side, the traits of conceit and cockiness are some of the absolute worst traits an individual can possess. These traits express insecurity, and a desire to gain attention. However, in their attempt to gain attention, their level of conceit and cockiness is such a turn-off to others, that they succeed in gaining attention, however, nothing but negative attention.

Super Achievers never have to try and gain attention simply because they are so excellent at what they do and humble in their approach and conduct, they naturally impress others.

Be humble! It's a wonderful and attractive trait to possess.

19)   **Compassion**

As I have outlined, Super Achievers possess extraordinary levels of mental and physical strength, passion for success and aggressiveness in their pursuit for greatness. However, among all these great traits of strength, there lies a softer, passive trait that in my opinion, may be just as powerful a trait if not more so. That trait is compassion.

Compassion is the ability to express or display sympathy, pity and understanding towards others. As you progress in your career, you will no doubt encounter individuals who are far less fortunate than you, having experienced great set-backs, failures and loss in their lives. Extending compassion and sympathy towards these individuals during their time of sadness or depression is a powerful trait to possess and in many cases, can actually be a healing gesture towards the individual.

Super Achievers always put themselves in other people's shoes and view life experiences, both positive and negative, through their eyes.

Super Achievers are compassionate and sympathetic towards the unfortunate, weak, depressed, aged and emotionally or physically hurt.

Why are they like this? Simply because they know, someday, they too may face, or become all of these things and will wish the same compassion, sympathy, understanding, support and pity on them.

20) Surround Yourself With ONLY Successful People

Remember this, you are judged by whom you associate with and are a product of your environment! This is a critical lesson to learn and understand.

Super Achievers understand the great importance of associating with only positive, moral, ethical and successful people in only positive, moral, ethical and successful environments. They know that negative, immoral, unethical and unsuccessful people will only douse their passion and enthusiasm in life, slow down their progress and journey to success and cause the development of poor habits, thoughts, words and deeds.

On the contrary, associating with only moral, ethical and successful people will do the exact opposite. It will ignite your passion and enthusiasm in life, speed up your progress to greatness, and cause the development of great habits, wonderful thoughts and positive words and deeds.

In the beginning of this book, I used the examples of a large number of movie stars, politicians, music stars and top executives who possess wealth and stardom, but not true success and happiness. These groups of individuals are perfect examples of those who get sucked into environments of immorality, unethical behavior, and negative and dangerous habits and associate with individuals who lead these types of lifestyles. In most cases, these individuals did not start off their careers or life paths with the intentions of living in this type of environment with these types of individuals. However, as I stated earlier, these individuals are and become a product of their environments. The more they lived in these environments and associated with these types of people, the faster they became just like them. And the worst part about becoming part of this type of unethical lifestyle is, once you're in it, it's virtually impossible to get out of it until the damage in your life is done.

Pick the right moral ethical environment and people to live in and with and your chances of achieving success and prosperity will increase ten fold.

21) Solution Oriented

There is one thing in life that is 100% guaranteed and that is that you will always face challenges and obstacles in both your personal and professional lives. There is no way around it. Super Achievers recognize this fact and focus all their efforts on becoming SOLUTION ORIENTED INDIVIDUALS AT ALL TIMES. They are constantly looking for answers and solutions to all of life's challenges and have a goal to become recognized as PROBLEM SOLVERS to all their peers and family members.

Life has a way of clearing a path to success for those individuals who are capable of not just facing and taking on life's challenges, but more importantly, recognizing all aspects of the challenge and deriving SOULTIONS that directly solve whatever the challenge or obstacle may be.

22) Never Take A Day For Granted

It is important that you understand that TIME is your most valued treasure. When today ends and tomorrow comes, this day is gone forever. Super Achievers recognize this fact and are thankful for each day of their lives. They know that they are free to use each day as they wish. They can waste it or maximize it! What they do each day is critical to their life's continued progress towards success because they are exchanging ONE DAY OF THEIR LIFE for it. Remember, when the day is gone, it's gone forever.

23)   Organization

Super Achievers are without question some of the most organized people on earth. They have every second of their day planned out working towards their goal.

You only have, 2,388,800,000 seconds in your life (if you live to 75) and they tick away without fail. You must live your life one second at a time and make sure that each second is being maximized to its fullest.

Being highly organized and in control of every second of your life ensures CLEAR THINKING, LESS STRESS, and overall control of their day to day lives.

24)   Responsible for Own Actions

If you choose the path of becoming a Super Achiever, the good news is that you are able to accept all of the accolades, rewards, financial gain and recognition that comes along with success. On the flip side, if you choose the path of becoming a Super Achiever, you also must accept the fact that you are responsible for your own actions and the repercussions of those actions, good or bad.

Super Achievers refuse to place blame on anyone and refuse to make excuses if things go wrong. They recognize the fact that as leaders, they are ultimately responsible for the good and bad.

They know that when they point a finger at someone, there are three fingers pointing RIGHT BACK AT THEM.

25) Patience

The phrase "PATIENCE IS A VIRTUE" is one of the most under-rated in the English language. Possessing high levels patience in all areas of your life is one of the most important traits any individual can have. Unfortunately, people's relentless pursuit of success, monetary gain and life advancement has created an environment of extreme impatience. People expect good things to happen now! If not now, tomorrow, next week, or at the latest, next month. Unfortunately, the reality is most good things in your career and personal life occur over longer periods of time through hard work, persistence and dedication.

That being the case, possessing patience in obtaining your success will not only enable you to stay calm, focused and have peace of mind, but it will also remove any levels of stress and discouragement associated with good things in life taking time to materialize.

Super Achievers understand that they CAN NOT RUSH SUCCESS. They understand that success happens in DIFFERENT WAYS, THROUGH DIFFERENT DOORS, WITH DIFFEENT PEOPLE AND MOST NOTICABLY AT DIFFERENT TIMES. Understanding this, they simply focus all their time, energy, thoughts, and attitude on taking action and the necessary steps to attain their desired goals.

The important thing to remember in life is that WITH PATIENCE, SUCCESS WILL FIND THEM!

26) Practice Constant Improvement

One of the most important habits to possess as a Super Achiever is to spend each and every day of their lives attempting to better themselves and improve their abilities in all areas of their lives.

Most Super Achievers I know strive to increase their knowledge in their careers or industries, expand their mind, learn new information, stay in tune with the world and current affairs, and increase their overall intelligence. While through the natural maturing and aging process, many of the improvements will eventually take place to some degree. However, the difference between the average person and Super Achievers is that Super Achievers REFUSE to wait through the aging process to improve and expand in all these areas. They understand that in order to attain and maintain Super Achiever status, they must fast forward the improvement process in all critical areas of their life NOW to stay ahead of the rest of the world.

How do Super Achievers improve in all areas of critical importance? They:
a) Daily read industry, career and field publications.
b) Listen to motivational and inspiration tape series.
c) Use the power of the Internet to explore for more and more information.
d) Attend business and industry seminars and conventions.

By improving in all the critical areas of their lives, years ahead of the average person, the chances of bypassing the majority of average people on your way to the highest levels of success you can attain are improved exponentially.

27) Fit For Life

Super Achievers understand that without excellent physical energy and strong health, they will be incapable of generating the personal energy required to attain unlimited levels of life success. Therefore, it is critical that you incorporate an organized, dedicated and consistent exercise routine that becomes part of your everyday life as well as a healthy diet.

When you feel healthy, look healthy and possess high levels of physical fitness, you naturally create a presence for yourself of success, prosperity and knowledge. You feel good about yourself, which feeds your self-esteem and confidence level, allowing you to perform and conduct yourself with the highest levels of integrity and professionalism.

You have been blessed with only one body. Make sure you treat it well. Without it, your chances of success are severely diminished.

28)   <u>Excellent Listening</u>

Super Achievers are excellent listeners. In their eyes, God gave them two ears and one mouth for a reason. To listen twice as much and they talk. Why is becoming an excellent listener so important in life, business, and family?

1) You will learn more.
2) Understand more.
3) Gain knowledge and experience.
4) Obtain facts and information.
5) Allow for effective decision making.
6) Learn about people.
7) Allow others to voice their opinions.

If you listen in life twice as much as you talk, you will always be able to obtain whatever information you need to handle, all people, all situations and all challenges. The most powerful form of communication is listening! STOP TALKING AND LISTEN. You will be amazed at the wealth of information you obtain, which only makes you stronger.

29)   Giving & Generosity

Of all the traits I discuss in this book, the one trait that possesses more meaning and power than all others is giving. The power and ability to give of yourself to others, whether in time, support, or material or monetary ways will reap you more success and greatness than you ever imagined.

The LAW OF GIVING is simple yet incredibly powerful. It is "THE MORE YOU GIVE OF YOURSELF TO OTHERS, THE MORE YOU WILL INEVITABLY RECEIVE IN YOUR LIFE". This is a fact.

Ever notice when you do a favor for someone, as small and insignificant as it may be, inevitably, that person, within a very short period of time, responds back to you with some other positive gesture. That's the Law of Giving. When you give to another or extend a genuine helping hand of support, advice, or material object, that person naturally feels a desire to give something back to repay your gesture to him or her. This Law of Giving transcends itself into your entire personal and professional life.

You will be amazed at what you receive from others when you continually give to others. The rewards will be beyond your wildest dreams.

Super Achievers understand that giving of themselves in any fashion to another individual is the single greatest task they can accomplish in their lives.

A Super Achiever's ultimate goal is to find a way, each and every day, to help someone else by giving of their time, energy, capital, kindness, or generosity.

No other daily goal in your life will make you feel as successful, fulfilled or complete as an individual as giving of yourself.

One of life's greatest phrases is that you "can't hold a torch to light another's path, without lighting your own at the same time."

Give as much of yourself as you can muster and watch the rewards in life roll into you.

30) <u>Cherish Family</u>

At the end of each and every day, after all your running and gunning to achieve your goals, there is nothing that comes close on the priority scale than YOUR FAMILY. Super Achievers understand the enormous importance of a strong family bond and family unity. They know that in their lives, they will encounter good times and bad, highs and lows and at the end of the day, family will be there for them to celebrate with or cry with.

Friends will come and go; business associates will come and go. Family will always be your stronghold, sounding board, support group and loyal companion for most of your life.

Without family, life has very little meaning. CHERISH THEM WITH ALL YOUR HEART!

Tactics of Achievement

The Tactics of Achievement are equally important for you to LEARN, UNDERSTAND AND IMPLEMENT immediately into your life. They consist of fifteen powerful personal development skills that are essential for you to learn in order to be capable of achieving the elite levels of success and prosperity. The tactics will provide you with the mental, and inner strength, vision and motivation levels necessary to attain Super Achiever status.

Let's now learn the TACTICS!

I.   TACTIC #1: Goal Setting

Few things in life reach the mission critical level in an individual's life than developing a personal goal strategy for yourself. Super Achievers realize that goal setting allows them to take complete control of their personal and career lives and dictate the direction they want to go. They recognize the fact that it is simply not possible to realize a fraction of your potential until you realize and understand how to set and achieve goals for yourself. Simply put, without successfully established goals.....You're a goner!

The first thing to understand is that human beings are goal centered organisms. They are engineered to mentally move forward and achieve at all times. Although this is the case, not all individuals are successful is their attempt to goal set as they have no idea how to effectively do so.

One of the best way's to define true success is "WHEN GOALS MEET NATURAL TALENTS AND ABILITIES". That said, the key to succeeding in goal setting is to identify your specific unique strengths, abilities and talents that have been the cause of most of your success and use these as springboards to goal setting and attainment.

Before I get into the how to's of successful goal setting, it's important that you understand the three key ENEMIES OF SUCCESSFUL GOAL SETTING so they can be avoided.

Enemy #1 – Low Level of Desire To Attain Goal:

The only limitation that exists in goal setting is the question of HOW BADLY YOU WANT TO OBTAIN YOUR GOALS AND HOW WILLING YOU ARE TO PAY THE PRICE TO GET IT. A low desire level in attaining your goals will be the fastest way to ensure you won't attain them

When you know exactly what you want to accomplish, when you want to accomplish it and, MOST IMPORTANTLY, IT'S WRITTEN DOWN, there are NO LIMITATIONS!

Enemy #2 – Entering A Comfort Zone:

Humans are motivated by a need or a want that is not satisfied. Once a need or a want of any kind is satisfied, it no longer motivates them, which eliminates the emotions of passion and desire. Once passion and desire are eliminated, humans have a tendency to fall into a Comfort Zone. THIS IS WHERE PROGRESS STOPS! This comfort zone must always be avoided. How do we do this?

Simple, we must do two things. 1) Become GREEDY about attaining our goals and 2) Most Important, continually RESET YOUR GOALS HIGHER AND HIGHER each time a goal is attained. By resetting your goals, you will remove yourself from the comfort zone and re-establish the emotions of passion and desire to achieve the new goal.

It's important to know that humans are not born with preconceived limitations on what you can and can't accomplish. Limitations are things we learn. It is society that teaches us that we can't accomplish through words and criticism.

Enemy #3– Lack Of Clarity:

It is critical that you approach all your goal setting processes with EXTREME CLARITY! Without a clear and concise clarity in each and every goal you establish, you will be destined for failure.

Clarity in one's mind is driven by a portion of the brain that is responsible for screening out all information EXCEPT WHAT IS ESSENTIAL FOR YOUR SURVIVAL. An Example of this brain power of screening is when a person buys a new car or begin to express strong interest in a particular car; they all of a sudden begin to see that car all over the road everywhere you look, while before they bought the car, they never noticed it. Why is this happening? Because during this time frame, they have a CLEAR FOCUS AND MIND SET on that particular car and their brain

47

begins to screen out all external information while driving except for that car.

This works the same way for goals. Once you become focused on one specific goal and have a clear mindset towards that goal, its all you can think of. And, that's the frame of mind you need to achieve your goals.

So much that could help you achieve your goals and dreams is never noticed or utilized simply because you have not taught your brain to be clear on what's important.

Goal setting will create this clarity and allow you to take the immediate and necessary steps towards achieving your dreams.

Keys To Successful Goal Setting:

In 1979, Harvard University conducted a Goal Setting study where they asked 1,000 students if they were goal setters. The outcome was:

a) 3% had written down their goals.
b) 13% had goals but did not write them down.
c) The rest had no goals.

In 1989, ten years later, Harvard approached those same 1,000 students to find out their success level. They found that:

a) The 13% with goals, but who did not write them down, made 5x more money than the rest of the students in the study.
b) The 3% who wrote down their goals made 20% more than the rest of the students in the study.

IS GOAL SETTING WORTH IT???? I would say so.

Now that I hope you see the power of goal setting, there are a number of keys to successful goal setting that I would like to point out.

1) When setting your goals, the goals must be ACHIEVEABLE, SPECIFIC AND REALISTIC.

2) You must have a BURNING DESIRE TO ACHIEVE YOUR GOALS

3) Goals MUST BE WRITTEN DOWN. Goals that are not written down are not goals, THEY ARE JUST WISHES.

    a. Writing down your goals means you are committed and have clarity.
    b. Thinking you can keep all your goals in your head is an excuse to not write them down.
    c. Too many things occupy your mind on a daily basis to remember it all.

4) The day you COMMITT TO YOUR GOALS, you have already achieved them, however, they just haven't arrived yet.

5) Setting goals must be done with extreme discipline

6) Don't procrastinate with goal setting by waiting for specific dates to start.......START TODAY.

7) Make the decision today to goal set and take control of your life. Make everything you do bring you closer to achieving your goals.

8) Goals must be worth committing to.

Developing Your Goal Setting Plan

Before you begin to strategize or implement any goal setting strategy into your life, you must first establish a foundation and direction for yourself by developing what I call a **PERSONAL GOALS PORTFOLIO** in a number of key areas of your life. Without establishing this foundation, you will be like a ship on the ocean without a rudder, bobbing aimlessly in no specific direction.

These key areas of your life that create the Personal Goals Portfolio are called LIFE VALUES. There are ten essential Personal Values that make up your life that you need to focus goal setting plans around. They are:
1) *Spiritual Goals*
2) *Material Goals*
3) *Financial Goals*
4) *Career Goals*
5) *Family / Relationship Goals*
6) *Community Goals*
7) *Travel/Recreation Goals*
8) *Friends Goals*
9) *Fitness and Health Goals*
10) *Personal Goals*

How To Develop Your Goal Setting Plan

STEP 1: Step one in developing your goal setting process is to FIND A PLACE OF COMPLETE QUIET for 1-3 hours where you can concentrate and reflect on your true short term and long term goals and desires. This portion begins with developing a DREAM LIST. Your Dream List should be a listing, written down, of all your dreams and desires as if you had no limitations of resources, time, money, assistance, or knowledge. You must open your mind, let your mind run free. This type of thinking is called "BLUE SKY THINKING".

STEP 2: Step two in developing your goals is to create your own personal MISSION STATEMENT. This should be one paragraph that summarizes your life's ambitions in your career, personal life, spiritual life and family life. It's a statement that explains how you want people to see you.

STEP 3: Step three in developing your goals is to create your own personal LEGACY STATEMENT. This should be one sentence that answers the question, "What do I want to be remembered for in my life?"

STEP 4: Step four in developing your goals is to go back to the ten LIFE VALUES and write down what your goals are to each of them and a timeframe of when you would like to achieve each goal. And, you must write down all your goals to each Life Value IN 60 SECONDS! Any goal that takes you longer than sixty seconds to think of is not a true, passionate goal in your heart. It's the goals that come to mind in 10 to 60 seconds that are your true goals.

After answering all the ten Life Value goal questions, it's time to get down to the nitty gritty and prioritize the importance of all of the goals.

STEP 5: Step five in developing your goals is to go back to each answer from the ten Life Value questions and number each one according to its importance to you on a scale from one to three.

> 1) A score of 1 are those goals that are the most important goals in your life that need immediate attention and action.
>
> 2) A score of 2 are goals that are important but not immediate priorities in your life.
>
> 3) A score of 3 are goals that are least important goals in your life.

STEP 6: Step six in developing your goals is to now combine all the scores of 1's together, 2's together and 3's together on a GOAL PRIORITY

WORKSHEET. The worksheet should be divided into three separate columns, the first column for all the scores of 1, the second column for all the scores of 2 and the third column for all the scores of 3. Then, cut each column apart so you have three individual column goal sheets. LAMINATE EACH ONE.

STEP 7: Step seven in developing your goals is to take fifteen to twenty minutes each day to review each of your goal sheets, and take daily action on all goals until each of them are attained. It may take days, weeks, months or even years to achieve all of your goals. However, the key is to review, make progress and take action EACH AND EVERY DAY.

STEP 8: Step eight, and maybe the most important step is to make sure that once any goal is attained, you establish a new and HIGHER GOAL in whatever Life Value category you are working in. Remember, you never want to enter the COMFORT ZONE and lose the drive and desire.

Final Goal Setting Advice

- In order for your plans, goals and dreams to stay fresh, and updated, you must continually review and revise them, much like an oil change on a car.

- Always assess whether your goals are attainable. The highest levels of persistence will never help you attain an unattainable goal.

- Believe that if you don't attain a goal, you did not fail, time just ran out. Be flexible and extend your timeframe to achieve your goal.

- Those who do not set goals are doomed forever to work for those who do have goals.

- Don't put off your joy and happiness in life to achieve your goals. To so many people, goal settings mean that only someday, after they have achieved something great, will they be able to enjoy life. THIS SHOULD NOT BE THE CASE. There is a big difference in achieving to be happy and happily achieving.

- THE ULTIMATE GOAL: Each day, have a goal to find a way to help someone else by giving of your time, energy, capital, kindness or generosity. No other goal accomplished will make you feel as successful.

TACTIC #2: Power Of Thought

If there is only one thing that is emblazed in your mind from this book, and of course I hope that is not the case, let it be this.....No other factor will impact the course of your life, career, destiny or future as will your thoughts! Your mind and the thoughts that it generates each and every day are without question the single most powerful factor in the direction your life takes. You can use your power of thought to attain incomprehensible levels of success and happiness or, you can use it to attain incomprehensible levels of failure and sadness. You have the power right now to chose the manner in which you utilize your mind and the thoughts it generates, and this chapter is going to show you how to use it and educate you on the unlimited levels of greatness and happiness you can attain if you use your thoughts effectively.

A powerful phrase that sums up this belief in the strength of the power of thought is, "What lies behind us and what lies before us are tiny matters compared to what lies within us".

Most Super Achievers I have been in contact with understand, more so than the average individual, how truly powerful the power of thought is and how it can significantly impact their lives in immeasurable ways.

Super Achievers have the following thought process:

1) They have a strong belief that whatever they believe, with emotion and passion, will become their reality.

2) They not only believe they are capable of achieving their goals, but believe they deserve to achieve their goals.

3) They believe they are destined for success and greatness and nothing can or will ever stop them from achieving it.

4) They believe in positive self expectancy. They confidently believe and expect themselves to succeed and win NO MATTER WHAT!

5) They believe in dwelling on the things they want to accomplish and the successes they want to experience. They also know that unsuccessful people dwell on the negative.

6) They believe that whatever they dwell and concentrate on most of the time will grow and become a reality.

7) In turn, they also believe that the more they dwell on the negative of their misfortunes, the greater is their power to harm them.

While this belief system in the power of thought sounds enticing, developing this belief system does not happen overnight. Effort on your part must be put into developing this form of thinking in order for it to impact your world.

The first thing you need to do is build your beliefs of yourself and your future in your mind bit by bit using the thoughts and images you hold in your conscious mind day by day. You must not only believe, without a shadow of a doubt, what your future will hold, how your future will develop and the type of person you will become in your career, personal and family life, but you also must be able to actually see yourself, in your mind's eye, being that person you believe you will be.

Once you succeed in building this power of thought about yourself and become passionate about becoming the person you want to be , you will experience the following:

1) You will begin to see what would normally be major setbacks and challenges as mere molehills instead of mountains.

2) You will look at every setback or disappointment not as failure, but simply as a lesson in your life development towards greatness.

3) You will become creative and capable of finding unique ways and methods of getting what you need to achieve.

4) You will become solution oriented. Focused on finding answers to the things you can affect not dwelling on the things you can't change.

5) You will eliminate fear of progression and change.

6) You will feel confident in taking risks and challenges.

7) You will develop the 'whatever it takes' attitude.

8) The more success you get, the more success you will want. This will continue to drive you towards meeting all your goals.

9) You will become an INVERSE PARANOID. A person who believes that the world is conspiring to do you good.

As you can see, the power of thought is, well, POWERFUL. The more you continue to turn your power of thought towards a mind frame of success, greatness and striving to achieve your each and every goal, the closer you come to actually attaining those goals. The key is to strengthen your power of thought about yourself and continually see yourself becoming the person you want to be ON A DAILY BASIS. **The more you believe, the more you will achieve! It's that simple**.

Eliminating Negative Thoughts

One of the most effective ways of strengthening your power of thought is by ELIMINATING ALL YOUR NEGATIVE THOUGHTS. That's right, you can actually replace all of your negative thoughts you have about yourself, your personal and your professional life with positive thoughts if you make a conscious effort to do so. How, you ask? Well, you first need to understand that your conscious mind can only hold ONE THOUGHT AT A TIME, positive or negative. You have the ability to consciously choose the level of quality of those thoughts whether they be positive or negative.

Those people who choose to continually process negative thoughts in their minds live a life filled with just that, NEGATIVITY. You may know some people like this. All they talk about is how miserable and discouraged they are with their current quality of life, education, career path, family, job and anything else they can find to complain about. You will find that most of these people, if they do not make a conscious effort to replace their negative thoughts with positive ones and redirect their thinking towards improving their life direction will remain in this negative state most of their lives.

By choosing to eliminate all negative thoughts from your mind, you will put yourself in a position to deliberately select and insert positive thoughts, in replacement of those negative thoughts, that will steer your life's path towards areas of success, forward progress and prosperity.

Remember, you are what you believe you are, you will achieve what you believe you can achieve and you will fail at what you believe you will fail at. Success and failure are in your hands. Believe you will succeed and YOU WILL!

In the early 1980s, the University of Massachusetts at Amherst conducted a COSTRUCTIVE THINKING STUDY using two groups of subjects. One group consisted of individuals that could be considered Super Achievers in their careers and personal lives and a second group of individuals that were considered average or under achievers. The study's focus was to report the difference in the thinking styles of the two groups. The conclusions were as follows:

1) SAs believe they will earn more money in their careers and ultimately become financially independent. . **AND THEY DO!**

2) SAs believe they will have prosperous family lives filled with peace and harmony. . **AND THEY DO!**

3) SAs believe they will enjoy more life success and find more purpose in life. . **AND THEY DO!**

4) SAs believe they will enjoy greater work success and work more efficiently in their jobs. . **AND THEY DO!**

5) SAs believe they will have more social success and have more friends. . **AND THEY DO!**

6) SAs believe they will be able to deal with failure, rejection or disapproval better than the average individual. . **AND THEY DO!**

7) SAs believe in ACTION ORIENTED THINKING. They believe in always moving ahead, progressing and getting the job done so they can move to the next action task. . **AND THEY DO!**

8) SAs believe they have the power to control the outcomes of their lives due to their positive and passionate approach to life, their families and careers. . **AND THEY DO!**

9) SAs DO NOT BELIEVE IN SUPERSTITIOUS THINKING. They believe in always having control of their life's outcomes. **AND THEY DO!**

10) SAs believe not achieving their goals IS NOT FAILURE, but a learning experience to be applied another day to an even greater opportunity.

11) SAs believe they are exceptional planners and highly organized, allowing them to plan out their entire life and career path. **AND THEY ARE!**

12) SAs believe in searching for new opportunities and experiences. They are able to confidently leave their comfort zones to progress to the next level of their lives. **AND THEY DO!**

If there is one thing that you learn and take away from this book, make it be the understanding that your mind and what you believe about yourself and your future will, more than any other factor, determine the level of success and happiness you achieve in your life. Commit to yourself RIGHT NOW that you will work on developing the power of positive thought into your every day life.

TACTIC #3: Positive Thinking

In the last chapter, I discussed the critical importance of developing the power of thought into your life. This chapter will focus more on the actual process of POSITIVE THINKING and the important role it will play in your life.

The first, and most important element to being able to possess a Positive Mental Attitude (PMA) is possessing a strong and positive SELF CONCEPT. Having a strong Self Concept is viewing yourself, your world, your family and your relationships with the highest regard. You not only believe in yourself, what you stand for and what you strive for, but you also view the people in your world the same way. Remember, as we stated earlier in this book, SA and highly successful and prosperous individuals have a tendency to be magnets to each other. If you view yourself with the highest regard, chances are you will view the relationships in your life also with the highest regard.

The higher your self concept, the greater your effectiveness and performance will be in all areas of your life. Remember, you can't perform higher than the level of your beliefs. Limit your belief in what you can achieve and you can be sure that your level of success and prosperity in life will also be limited. You are what you think you are, you're only as good at what you do as you think you are and you will become the person you believe you will be.

When you possess a PMA, and incorporate a PMA into each and every day of your life, your beliefs in yourself, your relationships and your future BECOME REALITY. You must always be thinking that THE BEST IS YET TO COME and dwell on anything and everything that you want to achieve and become. And, when what you believe is the best at a particular time in your life does come true, believe that now there is something even better to come next. Always raise the bar with your positive thinking once what you believed was the best occurs. This raising the bar method will always ensure that you never stop improving, advancing, and reaching greater and greater heights.

It's important to remember that YOUR LACK of a consistent positive mental attitude WILL DEFEAT YOU AND CREATE SETBACKS faster than any competitor, failure or mistake. A PMA must become part of your every day life.

Here's a PMA exercise that, if you're serious about achieving Super Achiever status, you will take part in every week of your life.

Pick a specific time and place each week that you can set aside five minutes and total peace and quit. At that specific time and place, repeat the following to yourself and truly believe in what you are saying.

1) I will never give up trying to attain my goals.

2) I will accept that failure and making mistakes is ok and learn from them.

3) I will not dwell on the negative or things I am not in control of.

4) I will accept that all things I believe are possible.

5) I will be responsible for all my actions, positive or negative.

6) I will develop my own good luck by making things happen.

7) I will do all important things that have the greatest reward right now.

8) I will live my life with honesty, integrity, kindness, and generosity and know that if I do, all things will go my way.

9) I will focus on doing good for others knowing that only good will come back to me.

10) I am not afraid to lose before I am victorious.

11) I will treat my body mentally and physically as though it is my temple.

12) I will understand that the better I get, the more I realize how much better I can continue to get.

Your daily mantra should be PMA every day! Live with PMA and watch how wondrous events and wonderful people begin to materialize in your life.

TACTIC #4: Visualization

You know the old expression SEEING IS BELIEVING? Well, no expression could be more correct.

In order to become the person you want to be and succeed in accomplishing your most desired goals and dreams, it is critical that you **SEE YOURSELF DOING SO.**

You must actually see yourself doing, being or achieving whatever it is you want to achieve through your mind's eye. You must see it **EXACTLY AS YOU WANT THE OUTCOME**. By doing this, you will automatically begin to bring the outcome to reality. Envision yourself actually operating on a patient's heart if you desire to be a surgeon, speaking to a jury if you dream of being an attorney, batting at home plate in Yankee Stadium if you desire to be a pro baseball player.

You may ask yourself, how can this be or how can this happen? Well, the mind has a tough time distinguishing between real experiences and simulated ones. By actually visualizing your goals being achieved in your mind's eye, your mind begins to interpret this visual signal as potentially being reality. By programming your mind into thinking this way, you begin to take all the necessary steps and meet the necessary people required to make the desire become reality.

It's a common practice on the part of most Super Achievers in business, sports or family life to use powerful visualization techniques whether preparing for a major sales presentation, performing an operation, giving a presentation to a large group or handling serious personal matters. By seeing themselves actually doing the thing they are preparing for, they are able to reduce stress, be more controlled and organized and avoid mistakes.

Understand that you are only limited by your vision of what you can do or achieve. You must envision BIG DREAMS AND GOALS. Only visualizing big dreams gives you the passion, drive, desire and motivation necessary to obtain your highest level of success.

There is one thing that **YOU MUST AVOID** when using visualization techniques. You must avoid **PAST FAILURES OR SHORTCOMINGS**. By visualizing these negative events in your life, you will only begin to program your mind for more of the same. Hit the ERASE BUTTON on all past failures and focus on seeing yourself achieve, succeed and improve in whatever your hearts content.

IF YOU CAN SEE IT, IT CAN BE!

TACTIC #5: Affirmation

The power of the spoken word can be both enlightening and devastating. Words spoken to you by others can inspire to the greatest levels and also demoralize to the lowest levels. What you say to others and what is said to you by others can dramatically change lives. This being fact, words that you SAY TO YOURSELF can also inspire or demoralize and change the course of your life. Motivating and inspiring yourself through your own words is called affirmation. Affirming the desires, goals and accomplishments you want to attain will build your sub-consciousness into actually believing that they can be or have been attained. Continually affirming to yourself positive thoughts that pertain to achieving your goals and desires will assist in enhancing your motivation, dedication and desire levels.

Two of the most powerful words in the English language are "I AM". By beginning each affirmation with "I AM", you are programming your sub- consciousness to understand that whatever words follow the "I AM" is reality. By saying..."I am the greatest Doctor there is" or I am the finest attorney in the court system or I am the kindest and most generous mother, you are developing your sub-conscious mind to actually believe what it is you are saying. By believing this, your subconscious mind will begin to set the path on doing whatever is needed to actually become what you are affirming you are.

One way to begin affirming your goals is to think about what you want to be, do or achieve, then say to yourself "I AM _____, and fill in the blank with your goal. Repeat this affirmation every day or every chance you have until your goal is attained. You will be amazed how much faster you will achieve your goals once you start to affirm that you will.

An even more powerful exercise you can take part in is the combining of Visualization and Affirmation in the same exercise. HERE IS A VISUALIZATION AND AFFIRMATION EXERCISE FOR YOU.

  1) Purchase a standard 5x7 notebook

2) On the top half of the page, write or type a Goal Affirmation. Example, "I AM THE GREATEST PITCHER IN THE MAJOR LEAGUES (Affirmation)

3) On the bottom half of the page, place a picture or magazine cutout of either you or a Super Achiever doing the same thing you affirmed above. Example, a picture of Roger Clemens pitching on the mound.

By affirming that you are the greatest pitcher in the Major Leagues and then visualizing yourself as great as Roger Clemens, one the history's greatest pitchers, you begin to program your mind to become as great as he is. You can do this same exercise whatever your goal is, whether it be material, business or family. Just be sure that the visual portion of the page portrays you or the material thing you desire as the best or finest there is.

Do this exercise each and every day and watch your desires and goals begin to materialize before your eyes.

On the flipside, you must also avoid the use of what I call FAILURE PHRASES. These are common phrases that cause you to admit defeat and failure and closes the door on any possibilities or opportunities of success. Examples of failure phrases that you must avoid are:

1) "I can't do it".
2) "It won't work".
3) "I can't figure it out yet".
4) "It's too hard for me".
5) "It will never happen".

These phrases will fill your mind and sub-conscious with thoughts of failure and defeat that will hinder you and de-motivate you as you try to attain your goals. You must avoid these phrases and CHANGE YOUR ATTITUDE to keep the opportunity door open. You can do this two ways.

Method One-Convert the phrase into a positive. Example

1) Change "I can't do it" to "I can or will do it".
2) Change "It won't work" to "It will or can work".
3) Change "I can't figure it out" to "I can or will figure it out".
4) Change "It's too hard for me" to It's no problem for me".
5) Change "It will never happen" to "It will happen".

By changing these phrases to a positive affirmation, you are conditioning your mind to accept the fact that you will achieve, succeed or accomplish your goal and that failure is not an option for you.

Method Two- Simply add the word "YET" to the end of each Failure Phrase. Example:

1) "I can't do it YET".
2) "It won't work YET".
3) "I can't figure it out YET".
4) "It's too hard for me YET".
5) "It will never happen YET".

By adding YET to the end of every failure phrase, you not only keep the door of opportunity and achievement open, but you change your mindset into believing that you still have more time to attain or achieve your goal. The word YET creates DELAYED SUCCESS. Delayed success is attaining success, but taking just a little more time to do it. The YET keeps the timeframe to succeed open-ended and gives you the extra time you need to continue to take the steps required to succeed.

TACTIC #6: Organization

Once you reach Super Achiever status, and you will, you will more than likely find that you are busier than you ever were in your life. Whether you reach this level in your career or family life, your Super Achiever status will naturally bring you more responsibility, more opportunities and more thought processing that needs to be managed. This being the case, it is critical that you become extremely organized in your mind, thought processes, planning process, office and desk setup, surrounding environment, and your personal/home environment.

A cluttered, disorganized mind, office, desk, home and thought process will only make it more difficult for you to have clarity and focus in making the right decisions and taking the right actions in your day to day life.

A cluttered, disorganized world will lead towards less progress, less effectiveness, lower productivity, increased confusion, and overall poor performance in all you do.

Super Achievers realize the importance of incorporating extreme levels of organization into every aspect of their life if they expect to perform and achieve at the highest levels consistently.

Here are some POWER TIPS on developing an organized world for yourself. These are what the Super Achievers do on a daily basis:

1) **PLAN FOR THE FUTURE TODAY.** Always plan your next day, week or month schedule, to do's, responsibilities, chores or calendar as far in advance as possible. This will allow you to plan and prepare effectively and avoid last minute scrambles for information.

2) **DO ONE ACTIVITY AT A TIME TO COMPLETION.** One of the biggest causes of disorganization in the mind is taking on too many projects or tasks at once and never completing any of them. As I stated above, as you get to Super Achiever status, you will become busier than you ever imagined. That's why it is important to do one task or project at a time until completed

and then move on to the next important task...IN PRIORITY ORDER OF COURSE. By dealing with one task at a time or completing as much as you can at any given point, you will be more able to focus and concentrate on the task at hand, which will ensure that it is being handled in the correct manner. Your mind will be clear on the objective in front of you and will not be distracted by other tasks that you have partially on your mind. Taking this approach may make it seem like you are less busy and productive due to your low level of stress and confusion. But believe me, you will be 100% more productive, effective and efficient if you take this approach.

3) **HAVE ONE THING ON YOUR DESK AT A TIME.** Whenever you are working at a table or desk, make an effort to have ONE THING OR TASK ON YOUR DESK AT ONE TIME. This will allow you to focus on that one task and avoid being distracted by other material lying around you. A cluttered desk or work area creates a cluttered mind. And, a cluttered mind leads to inefficiency, confusion and mistakes.

4) **FIND PEAK ENERGY TIME (INTERNAL PRIME TIME).** In order to maximize your level of organization and focus on one task at a time until completion, you must feel fresh and energized physically and mentally. It's important that find your PEAK ENERGY TIME of the day. Peak Energy Time is a period of the day that you feel best, both mentally and physically. All individuals have this, but it occurs at all different times. Some people do their best and most efficient work very early in the morning while others work better at night (Although, the majority of people I have worked with work best in the morning after a good night's sleep). Find YOUR PEAK ENERGY TIME and schedule all of the tasks, responsibilities or work that needs high levels of organization and focus at THIS TIME OF THE DAY.

5) **REMAIN FLEXIBLE.** As organized and prepared as you may be, interruptions and distractions will occur. DO NOT LET THESE INTERFERE WITH YOUR FOCUS. Be flexible, handle the distractions, dispose of them if possible, and then get back to your tasks with the same focus and organization you had before the interruption.

6) **ALWAYS DO WHAT IS MOST IMPORTANT.** Being organized is critical and key to performing at high productivity levels, however, if you are not ALWAYS DOING WHAT IS MOST IMPORTANT AT THE TIME, you will never be as efficient as you need to be to become a Super Achiever. Always ask yourself, "Is what I am doing now the most efficient use of my time at the moment to reach my goal?" If the answer is NO, stop what you are doing and do the thing you feel is the most important use of your time.

7) **PRACTISE THE ART OF "TIO" (TOUCH IT ONCE).** This habit is one of the most important factors to being organized. As I already outlined, having one thing on your desk at a time is one of the most important factors to being organized. A second important factor is working towards TOUCHING ONE TASK OR RESPONSIBILITY ONCE. I don't necessarily mean physically touching, but touching in the sense that you work on a task or paperwork ONCE until completion and move on to the next task. Do your best to avoid constantly going back to a task over and over again. Handle or touch all your tasks or responsibilities ONLY ONCE. This will cause you to remain organized and efficient without having numerous projects or responsibilities always partially completed.

8) **PERSONAL ORGANIZATION HOUR.** Each week, find one hour, usually Sundays before the school or work week begins, to plan your week out. This will be your PERSONAL ORGANIZATION DAY. Planning your week out in advance will be a major step in the right direction in remaining organized and focused on all that you need to do week to week. Not planning your week out in advance will only lead to disorganization, confusion and last minute RUSH SESSIONS to get things done. By knowing exactly where you

need to be, what needs to get done, and when things need to be completed, you will become highly organized and efficient in all you do.

9) **GET A MINI TAPE RECORDER.** There is no way any Super Achiever is capable of remembering everything he or she needs to do on a daily basis by memory alone. As powerful as the brain is, it is not possible for it to remember each and every bit of data that comes into it every day as thousands of thoughts and ideas are being processed daily. This is why it is so important that you purchase a mini tape recorder that will enable you to record all the important thoughts and ideas that surge into your mind on a daily basis. Too many times, thoughts and ideas come into the mind that are critical to your daily responsibilities only to be forgotten and lost as new streams of information, ideas and thoughts come into the brain. Don't be foolish and try to remember it all. IT'S SIMPLY IMPOSSIBLE! Get a tape recorder and guarantee yourself that you will never forget to do another thing.

TACTIC #7: Time Management

In the last chapter, I discussed the importance of being organized in your day to day tasks and responsibilities and how important this is to you becoming a Super Achiever. Part of being successful with organization is have strong TIME MANAGEMENT skills. Time Management is having the ability to organize, daily, weekly, monthly and annual responsibilities in a PRIORITIZED (KEY WORD) fashion based on the most important tasks that provide the greatest reward or avoid the greatest setbacks.

I can not stress enough how important it is to ALWAYS BE DOING THE MOST IMPORTANT THING, TASK OR RESPONSIBILITY at all times. It is the only way to ensure that you will be progressing in your life, career or schooling in the most efficient fashion.

You have heard many people say, I am sure, "There is just not enough time in the day to get it all done". NOT SO, there is plenty of time in each day. The problem is most people do not prioritize their time or maximize the time they have to use to its fullest.

There is a law of life called the LAW OF ALTERNATIVE CHOICE. This says that when you choose to do one thing, you are choosing NOT TO DO SOMETHING ELSE. Everything you do IS A CHOICE. Every day of your life, you have the power to determine WHAT YOU DO. You have only twenty–four hours in a day that you can spend at will. You can maximize your day being productive and making progress or you can stay in bed and get nothing accomplished. YOU HAVE THE POWER TO MAKE THIS CHOICE.

Before you make this choice, and I am sure you will make the right choice, remember:

1) Time can not be stretched out. As mentioned earlier, you only have twenty–four hours a day. And approximately eight hours of that time you are asleep. You must use each and every minute to its fullest.

2) Time is PERISHABLE AND IRREPLACEABLE. It can't be saved or stored. Once it' gone, it's gone forever, never to have again. Use it to its fullest.

It is the decisions on how you spend your time in your life that will truly determine your destiny. One right decision and effective use of your time can open up the flood gates of joy, success, prosperity, companionship and health, while one bad decision and poor use of your time can bring upon sorrow, depression, poverty, failure, solitude and poor health.

What you do each and every day is in your power. How you spend your time is in your power. Don't be irresponsible by wasting the precious gift of time that you possess. Use each and every moment to your advantage and life progress to Super Achiever status.

A great analogy for Time Management is the game of baseball. In baseball, victory is not determined by hits but by runs. Many times the team with the most hits loses due to their lack of success in scoring enough runs. Getting to third base does not give a team 3/4th of a run. The team members must cross home plate and **FINISH WHAT THEY SET OUT TO ACHIEVE TO WIN.** Tasks are the same thing. Getting started on a task and carrying it forward is fine, but until the task is completed (RUN SCORED) you have not truly accomplished anything worth merit. Possessing effective Time Management skills will ensure that you never hit singles, doubles or triples, but always score runs for yourself.

Before I begin to educate you on powerful Time Management skills, I would like to point out the single biggest reason why individuals fail at being successful at Time Management. It's called the "SET ASIDE FOR LATER" principle (SAFL). The words say it all. The majority of individuals, non Super Achievers, begin working on their tasks and responsibilities and then SET IT ASIDE for another task or responsibility that comes along without ever completing it. This is the same thing as leaving base-runners stranded on base in a ballgame without ever scoring a run. It's a proven fact in baseball that the teams with the highest percentage of leaving base runners on base are, on average the worst teams in the major leagues. DO YOU WANT TO BE THE WORST PERFORMER IN YOUR LEAGUE? If not, and I would imagine you absolutely do not want that, incorporate the following Time Management skills into your life immediately!

Once you do, you will begin to score runs and cross home plate more times than you could have ever imagined.

KEYS TO SUCCESSFUL TIME MANAGEMENT

The following Time Management skills are ten of the most powerful skills you could ever incorporate into your life. For each one you embrace, your chances of attaining success and Super Achiever status will increase dramatically. For each one you fail to embrace, your chances of reaching Super Achiever status will be lessoned. As I said earlier. **YOU HAVE THE POWER TO CHOOSE HOW YOU SPEND YOUR TIME.**

1) You must begin with CLARITY, A PLAN AND ORGANIZATION. The more complete and clear your plans are and the more organized you are in your thoughts, the greater your chances of success. Studies have proven that for every one minute of planning you conduct, you save five minutes of execution time. That's a 500% return on your time! Think you'll be effective and productive? I certainly do.

2) Make the DECISION TO START A TASK. Many times, the greatest inhibitor of not completing tasks and responsibilities is simply the fact that people never MAKE THE FINAL DECISION TO TAKE ACTION NOW on a particular task. They ponder whether they should start it, question whether they should start something else and many times come up with any excuse not to start it because they're lazy. The first order of business when starting a Time Management schedule is MAKE THE DECISION TO ACT NOW on the thing you feel is most important and don't allow yourself to be distracted or diverted into doing something else. Unless of course, it is more important!

3) Develop your own Time Management Priority System that includes doing the urgent and important tasks first as those tasks are the ones that will benefit you the most! There is no magic time management solution. You must develop a system that works for you and is tailored to your daily routine of tasks and responsibilities.

4) Before you begin a new task or responsibility, review and assess each of them according to the reward factor as well as the damage it could do if left alone and not completed.

5) Remember that there is never enough time to do EVERYTHING! But there is always enough time to do the important things. It's up to you to identify the important things and spend your time focusing on them while weeding out the non important things and pushing them out to a later date.

6) Practice NEATNESS. Neatness and order in life is Heaven's Law. Ask yourself the question, "Are you neat and orderly in your life and surroundings?" Look at your desk, room, car, house, office, closet, knapsack, briefcase, and suitcase and ask yourself, "What kind of person works here or lives here?" "Is this the house, office, desk or room of a Super Achiever?" You know what to do if the answer is no. GET NEAT AND ORDERLY! Being neat and orderly will cause you to feel more productive and allow you to plan your time management schedule with a clear and focused mind.

7) Focus on TIME SENSITIVE Responsibilities. In many cases, you may have numerous important tasks and responsibilities that need your attention and you're having difficulty deciding which one to start with. Your answer is TIME SENSITIVITY. In all cases, your tasks and responsibilities will all have an associated TIME OF COMPLETION date associated with them. When numerous important tasks are at the forefront, decide to take action on the task or responsibility that needs to be completed in the soonest timeframe. Then, take action on the next time sensitive task date and so on. By taking

this Time Sensitive approach, you will always complete your tasks and responsibilities on time and efficiently avoiding last minute RUSH SESSIONS.

8) Take care of and pay attention to those people who can always assist you with your tasks and responsibilities and most seriously impact the accomplishment of your priorities. THIS IS REAL IMPORTANT. Whether you're in school, at work or in a family setting, there are always those individuals who can make your life easier by assisting you with your tasks and responsibilities. It could be a teacher, professor, supervisor, parent or even friend. Whoever it is, identify who that person is and give that individual the appropriate attention, kindness, politeness and respect AT ALL TIMES. Incredible levels of success can be attained if you associate yourself with the right SUPPORT PEOPLE. Make use of them.

9) At the same time that you are identifying those individuals who can assist you in your priorities, be aware of those people who can be a deterrent to you in attaining or completing your tasks AND AVOID THEM. As you get closer and closer to achieving Super Achiever status, you will begin to see more and more people who are lazy, slow, procrastinators or counter productive in all they do. If you make the mistake of associating yourself with these type of people or worse, identifying them as potential support people, you will experience nothing but delays, set backs and problems. STAY AWAY FROM THESE PEOPLE!

10) Handle every piece of paper ONCE. (DSWI–DO SOMETHING WITH IT NOW). Since the beginning of computer technology, the internet and electronic files, the world believed more and more that the need and use of paper would diminish. Then the phrase, "The Paperless World" was coined. Well, let me be the first to tell you that paper is NOT GOING ANYWHERE! You will continue to utilize paper all throughout your schooling and career and it will continue to remain as one of the most distracting, confusing and biggest waste of your time management scheduling UNLESS YOU ORGANIZE IT. There are four things you can do with every single piece of paper you encounter.

    a. **TOSS IT:** The best Time Management tool for paper is THE GARBAGE PAIL. More distractions and confusion are caused by excess paper laying all over your work space than any other factor. Get rid of all paper that is not important, and newspapers, books or magazines that do not relate to your tasks and responsibilities at hand. You will be amazed at the level of clarity and focus you experience when you rid your desk or work environment of excess paper.

    b. **REFER IT:** Ask yourself the question, "Is there someone else who should be handling or using this piece of paper?" If so, delegate it to a roommate, co-worker, family member or even professor or boss.

    c. **ACTION IT:** Actually take immediate action on it UNTIL COMPLETION!

    d. **FILE IT:** Ask yourself the question, "Will I ever really need this piece of paper or information again? "What if I can not ever find this piece of paper or information again. Can I live without it?" If you can live without it, perform the TOSS IT method above. If you can't live without it, file it in a place where you know you will be able to find it again.

11) Plan out your week on Sundays and review the next day's calendar of events the night before. I know I touched on this earlier, but I wanted to explain why it is so important. When you plan out your next day' tasks and responsibilities the night before, you insert your thoughts, todo's and plans into your subconscious mind. When you're sleeping, your subconscious mind goes right to work on your plans, feeding your mind with ideas, insights, planning, focus and clarity. When you wake up, your mind is primed to attack your tasks and responsibilities with 100% focus, determination, knowledge and desire that will stay with you all day.

12) Nail down what your INTERNAL PRIME TIME is and do your most difficult or creative work, tasks, chores and responsibilities at that time of the day.

13) Incorporate powerful WORK HABITS into your day that will improve or enhance your quality of work:

   a. Start work or arrive to class a few minutes earlier, before other students or employees do. This is usually a very quiet period of time without distractions that will enable you to prepare and concentrate on the events to follow.

   b. Work through normal lunch times. Lunch time, when most people go to lunch between 12:00pm and 1:30pm is one of the best times to remain working. While most are eating, your surrounding environment usually becomes peaceful and quiet. Remain working on your tasks until the lunch crowd returns, then you go to lunch. Believe it or not, now that you're at lunch when everybody else is back working, you will once again have an additional hour of peace and quiet.

   c. Staying a bit later after class or work is also a good time to continue working on your tasks and responsibilities. Again, your surrounding environment remains peaceful and quiet.

d. Work wisely but briskly. Remember, you only have so much time in a day to accomplish your priorities. Work at a brisk pace and in control so you can finish and move onto the next task at hand. Your goal here is to ensure you are generating the highest work output possible in the time you have allocated.

e. In some cases, being a perfectionist can be a negative. Make sure that you are doing your best work on your tasks possible. However, don't sacrifice the completion of a task for a level of perfection that may be too difficult to attain. Use your judgment on when to complete a task and when to hold on to it for improvement.

f. Recognize when you have put in enough time and effort on a task and give yourself a rest. Overworking and burning yourself out can have devastating effects on your journey to Super Achiever status. When your mind is tired, eyes getting sleepy or blurry or you're just not thinking with any level of sharpness, end the day and pick up on it the following day after a good night's sleep. You will see that you will wake up as fresh and creative the next day.

14) Know your life's priorities! As you strive to attain Super Achiever status in life, it's important that no matter how busy you get, no matter how many added tasks and responsibilities you take ownership in, don't ever let your life get so overwhelmed that you lose sight of your true life priorities.

Ask yourself the question, "If I found out today that I only had five more days to live, how would I spend my time?" I guarantee you it would not be in class, at work, in the office or in a hobby. You would spend every second of the last five days with the people you love. Your family, mother, father, sister, brother, son, daughter, best friend or grandparents. I say this because I never want you to get the impression that the material in this book is the driving force of your life and future. While it is all important in moving your future in the right, successful direction, don't let the material in this book blind you of your life's true priorities. They will always come first.

There is an old saying about time that I believe sums up how important your time is in life.

"Time is the only thing that can never be retrieved. One may lose and regain a friend, one may lose and regain money, an opportunity that was once spurned may come again, but the hours that are lost in idleness can never be brought back to be used in gainful pursuits."

TACTIC #8: Avoiding Procrastination

Perhaps the greatest gap in life is the one between KNOWING & DOING. It's called the PROCRASTINATION GAP.

It's truly amazing to me how many individuals have mastered the ART OF PROCRASTICATION. The Art of Procrastination is simply the **ART OF DOING NOTHING, ACHIEVING NOTHING and DECIDING ON NOTHING!** The procrastinators are experts in taking on tasks and responsibilities and never taking action on them to avoid some form of personal pain that would be associated with the tasks. What procrastinators don't realize is that the more they procrastinate to avoid personal pain, the more personal pain they actually bring upon themselves due to lack of performance and progress in their lives.

Procrastinators spend their life in their very own Twilight Zone, between thinking of doing and actually doing. They constantly analyze, ponder, rethink and never make progress or a decision. By not making decisions, they are better able to stay in control of the task or the responsibilities since they never come to completion, allowing them to move onto the next task. They'll make excuses constantly, but never offer any real answer or solution to the excuse. They simply delay, delay, delay. Phrases that most procrastinators say are:

a) I'm overwhelmed.
b) I have too many competing priorities.
c) I have a poor sense of urgency.
d) I do not have enough information.
e) I'll make too many mistakes.

In the eyes of the procrastinator, taking on the task may lead them to more work, more meetings, spending more money, being involved with other people they are not fond of or a list of hundreds more personally painful events. Therefore, to avoid these painful events, they simply do nothing. Or, best case, appear that they are working but doing so at a snail's pace, delaying the inevitable pain they are expecting. Do you know any procrastinators? I bet you do. Bottom line. **DON'T BECOME ONE!** Avoid procrastination at all costs. And, if you think you may be a procrastinator, DON'T REMAIN ONE. Being a procrastinator will sabotage your life, future, potential and career faster than anything you ever imagined.

There is a six point model for avoiding procrastination and becoming more decisive.

1) Give careful consideration and thought into all facts, opinions and information at your disposal regarding a task or responsibility. Being armed with this information will better enable you to make quick decisions.

2) Pay attention to your heart, gut and intuition. If something makes sense to you, but does not feel right in your gut, BEWARE. Your intuition, gut and heart are the most powerful decision makers you will ever know. Listen to them! Listening to your heart, gut and intuition will give you the confidence you need to make quick, and correct decisions in all your tasks and responsibilities.

3) Once you make a decision, don't second guess yourself. If you went with your gut, and you feel good about your decision, you've probably made the right moves. Too many important decisions will be made in your lives to waste valuable time lamenting and regretting your past decisions.

4) Act with the knowledge and confidence that you will probably make more good decisions than bad ones in your life and career. It's important to make sure you understand you can make mistakes and wrong decisions. It's OK! But just make sure to learn from them every time!

5) Always anticipate success, BUT NEVER BE AFRAID TO FAIL! Ever! Some of the greatest leaders, most successful individuals and famous personalities of our time have failed more than you could ever imagine.

6) Live by the phrase TAKE ACTION NOW. Ask yourself, "What will happen to me if I do not act now?" Then ask yourself, "What are the exciting possibilities or opportunities for me if I do act?"

7) Remember the most important two words to avoid procrastination....DON'T WAIT!

TACTIC #9: Forming Good Habits

Forming good habits in all areas of your life is essential to achieving success and prosperity in life. Good habits cover many areas of life such as ethical and moral behavior, good health and eating habits, good personal hygiene habits and a host of others. To summarize good habits, it is the general appearance or manner in which you conduct and carry yourself.

I'm sure you have some bad habits, maybe you smoke, overeat, use foul language, bite nails, are lazy, procrastinate etc. The reality is you will continue to behave and think the same way indefinitely unless you make a decision to change these habits. Super Achievers are capable of eliminating all of the negative habits and replace them with good habits that work towards propelling their life and career towards superior levels of success. You can do the same. But it will take a little work on your part.

You must first understand that the habits you make or break will make or break you! This Law of Habits pertains to all areas of your life. You must embrace the fact that in order to obtain your greatest potential in your personal and career life, you MUST FORM ONLY THOSE HABITS THAT WILL LEAD TO SUCCESS.

There are four essential areas of habits that you must focus on developing in a positive fashion. They are:

1) **HEALTH HABITS**: You have only one body that has a limited lease here on earth. Your body is your physical driving force for all you do. Keep it in tip top shape with healthy eating and exercise habits, free of negative habits such as smoking, drinking, drugs, and poor sleep and you will be able to accomplish everything you set out to achieve. Don't take care of your body and you will experience extreme physical set backs, injuries, illness, disease, laziness and mental and physical fatigue.

2) **THOUGHT HABITS:** You must dwell on the positive and affirm only optimistic thoughts. Visualize your successes and fill your mind with thoughts that feed your subconscious with images of success.

3) **CAREER HABITS**: You must goal set, be organized, use time management, plan in advance and constantly self improve with more knowledge, information, experience and skill sets.

4) **FAMILY HABITS**: Treat, speak and communicate with your loved ones with care and thoughtfulness. These people are your LIFE PRIORITIES. Treat them like they are the most important people on earth. Remember, if you only had five more days to live, you would spend every second with them.

Breaking BAD Habits

For those of you who have accepted the fact that YOU HAVE BAD HABITS, I'm sure by now you want to know how to break them. There is a seven step process to break these habits. Follow these steps and you can be assured that the habits will slowly drift away.

1) **TAKE SMALL STEPS**: Pinpoint the bad habits you want to break and plan out, in small steps, what you need to do to break them.

2) **TACKLE ONE BAD HABIT AT A TIME**: Don't try to break all your bad habits at once. You need to be able to focus all your energy towards breaking one bad habit at a time, them move on to the next. If you try to break more than one habit at a time, you will more than likely become overwhelmed, stressed out and irritable and fail to break any of the habits.

3) **TELL FAMILY AND FRIENDS YOU ARE TRYING TO BREAK A HABIT**: Aside from possibly receiving good advice on how to break

your habit, family and friends can be a powerful support mechanism that will encourage you and strengthen your resolve to break your habit. Aside from yourself, there is probably nobody else who wants you to break your habit more than your loved ones.

4) **KEEP A JOURNAL**: By keeping track of your progress ON PAPER, you will be able to SEE THE POSITITVE RESULTS of your bad habits being broken. Keep track of each consecutive day that you did not smoke, did not overeat etc. This process will also keep you accountable to yourself.

5) **SET A FIRM GOAL SCHEDULE**: Layout a specific goal and timeframe for the habit you want to break. Example; I will not use foul language for three straight days. Once that is accomplished, set a new goal to not use foul language for four straight days. This goal setting will organize your action steps and lead you to breaking your habit in quicker fashion as well as strengthen your commitment and dedication.

6) **ACQUIRE A REPLACEMENT HABIT**: Breaking a bad habit may leave a difficult void in our life. Replace it with a positive, beneficial or healthy habit that will fill that void. Example; when you stop smoking, start chewing gum. When you stop eating fatty foods, start replacing it with high protein, lean foods.

7) **REWARD YOURSELF**: As you progress in breaking your habits, reward yourself for your accomplishments. Give yourself a break!

DO THE THINGS FAILURES DON'T LIKE TO DO

The importance of STRONG HABITS was never made so clear than in a 1940 speech by a Prudential Insurance executive named Albert Grey during a meeting of the Million Dollar Round Table for top sales achievers at Prudential. According to Mr. Grey........

"The secret of success of every person who has ever been successful lies in the fact that they formed the habit of doing things that failures don't like to do. Mr. Grey claimed there is no difference between what failures don't like to do and what successful people don't like to do. The difference is, successful people discipline themselves to do what they don't like to do to get what they really want out of their career.
Every single qualification for success is acquired through habit. People form habits and habits form futures."

CHAPTER #3

Facing Fear & Failure

CHAPTER 3: Facing Fear & Failure

Facing and conquering your fears and accepting and dealing with failure are two of the most important elements of the journey to success you will need to deal with. Studies have shown that the single greatest cause of individuals not attaining their goals or desires is FEAR OF FAILURE or another form of FEAR associated with not attaining your goal. I can say, without a shadow of a doubt, if you have any form of fear that is associated with your dreams, desires or ultimate goals in life, you must face those fears now and defeat them or face the consequences of failure.

It is fear that....

1) Is the greatest single enemy of a person's potential.

2) Holds you back from taking risks and accepting challenges that lead to success.

3) Paralyzes taking action.

4) Causes you to dwell on the negative instead of the positive.

5) Causes you to dwell on what you can lose instead of what you can win.

6) Causes you to dwell on what will go wrong rather than what will go right.

Any form of fear in your journey to Super Achiever status will derail your progress and leave you limping along beaten and defeated. However, conquer your FEARS and be prepared to emerge victorious in anything you so desire. That's the power of conquering FEAR.

You may question whether you can conquer your fears. STOP QUESTIONING! You can and will conquer your fears and I will now show you how.

You must first understand what fear and failure really is. Everything you do is a result of an emotional decision and there exists two primary emotions that effect and motivate your behavior.

1) FEAR
2) DESIRE

Studies have shown that the majority of the American population make their decisions based on the emotion of FEAR. Fear of failure, loss of money, possessions, job, status, title, credibility and a host of others. Because of these fears, the majority of the American population remain in their comfort zones, never taking the smallest chances or risks in any area of their lives. This reason alone is why there are so few Super Achievers in America today. It's the Super Achievers who step out of their comfort zones, not afraid to fail or lose, and take the necessary chances and risks in life that will increase their chances of obtaining success and prosperity.

Put simply, whichever emotion or desire you concentrate on each and every day of your life, it is that which will grow and control your life. Dwell on success, constant improvement and attaining your goals and you will surely become a Super Achiever. Dwell on your fears and do nothing to defeat them, and you will surely fail.

That said, to eliminate fear you must:

1) Force yourself to concentrate on the things you desire and want to achieve at all times.

2) Attack the things you fear and you will defeat fear.

3) Eliminate all thinking of failure and fear from your mind. Once removed, your mind will never again understand how to fail at something. An interesting example of this concept actually comes

from the Bumble Bee. Aerodynamically, and physically the bubble bee should not be able to fly due to weight to wing span ratio. However, the bumble bee does not know this so it just continues to fly without ever thinking of failing to fly. Failure to fly is not part of the bumble bee's thinking process.

These are the action steps you must incorporate into your life that will be directly responsible for diminishing your fears to the point where your desires will take control over the direction of your life.

Failure: You must accept it, deal with it and learn from it

You will fail! How's that for a bold statement. Even after reading this book, and even if you applied every single trait and tactic taught, you will in someway at sometime fail at something. Now, get over it! It's no big deal. In fact, failure will become your best friend in life. How can this be, you ask? Here's how. When you fail, two things have more than likely happened.

1) You have taken a risk or made a change in your life that you perceived as a positive move forward, but may have been beyond your means to handle due to lack of experience, lack of support or knowledge. All I can say to this is CONGRATULATIONS! You have done the one thing that most unsuccessful individuals NEVER DO. Make a change or take a risk. The fact the you took the risk or made the change shows that YOU DO NOT HAVE FEAR to take on new opportunities and that you have extreme confidence in yourself and your abilities. By failing, you have become a stronger, more knowledgeable individual. Use this failure as a stepping stone to the next big thing in your life. Chances are, you will fail again, but I bet when you fail again, you will be far more successful and far more prosperous than you would have been without the failure.

The critical thing to do now is LEARN FROM THE FAILURE and apply the learning experience to similar circumstances that develop in your life. By doing this, you will NEVER MAKE THE SAME MISTAKE OR FAIL AT THE SAME THING AGAIN!

2) You set your goals, dreams and potential too high and maybe fell short of achieving them. Again, CONGRATULATIONS! You have once again proven your lack of fear and high confidence in yourself. View this not as a failure of achieving your goals, but simply that you ran out of time, and would have achieved the goal if you had more time.

It's always important to set your goals high. Very high. But not so high that it is unrealistic that you will achieve the goal. An example of this is a company whose upper management sets a realistic goal to generate $10,000,000 in sales in one year. However, the true Super Achiever companies set their goal and inform their sales people that the sales goal is $15,000,000 and use that as their target to shoot for. Now, if the company generates only $12,000,000 in sales, have they failed to meet their goal? Would you consider this a failure? Well, yes they did fail to meet their goal, but with $2,000,000 in sales higher than they realistically expected, is this a failure? I THINK NOT. They drove their sales force to believe that $15,000,000 was the goal and the sales force responded accordingly falling short of the goals but exceeding the realistic goal of upper management.

The point here is always MAKE FAILURE WORK FOR YOU. Shoot for higher goals than you expect and you just may be surprised how far you actually go.

In making failure work for you, do the following:

1) Understand that failure can be your best friend.

2) View all failures as mistakes and learn from them.

3) Be sure to apply the lessons you learned to all future situations and opportunities.

4) Avoid making the same mistakes that caused the failure again.

5) Understand that THE ONLY WAY TO TRULY DEFEAT FAILURE IS TO SUCCEED, SUCCEED AND SUCCEED. The more success and prosperity you taste, the more success and prosperity you want to taste! Success will transform your attitude into a win and succeed at all costs mentality. It will transform your mind and body to focus on one thing and one thing only; SUCCESS. It will re-motivate, re-dedicate, and instill a level of discipline towards taking the action and achieving success like you have never experienced.

6) Plow through times of failure without the slightest thought of failure. If failure occurs, ACCEPT IT, DEAL WITH IT, LEARN FROM IT, pick yourself up, dust yourself off and move to the next, even greater challenge.

Your daily motto should be FAILURE IS NOT AN OPTION. If you believe this with a passion, FAILURE WILL NEVER BE AN OPTION OR REALITY FOR YOU.

Failure: You're Not Alone.....Believe me

As I stated earlier, some of the most successful, wealthy, talented, and most respected people in America today have experienced significant failures in their lives before they reached Super Achiever status. It's because of their failures they were able to push on with passion and dedication to become the successes they became. The following is a listing of some of these people. I am sure you will be amazed at some of the names on this list and the ways in which they failed before they became Super Achievers.

> Theodore Geisel (Creater of Dr. Suess Books)-Dr. Seuss took his book to 20 publishers before the 21st accepted it.

> Thomas Edison made 3,000 attempts before he invented the light bulb.

> Studies have shown that the average millionaire has been broke 2-3 times.

> Babe Ruth struck out 1,330 times. One of the most in baseball history.

> Fred Astaire's first screen test review– "Can't act, bald and can dance a little."

> An expert said of Vince Lombardi– "He possesses minimal football knowledge and lacks motivation".

> Walt Disney was fired by a newspaper for lacking ideas. And, was bankrupt several times before building Disney.

> An early teacher review of Beethoven's musical talent– "Hopeless as a composer!"

➤ Baseball great Kirby Puckett, after being cut from a triple A farm team, was working on loading docks when the Minnesota Twins heard about him.

➤ After ET in 1982 and before Jurassic Park and Schindler's List in 1993, which all received academy awards, Steven Spielberg directed four major box office failures between 1985 and 1989. (The Color Purple, Empire of the Sun, Always and Hook).

➤ In 1991, home run king Mark Mcgwire had a disastrous season batting .201 with 22 home runs. This poor performance almost cost him his career.

➤ Drew Carey, star of the top sitcom The Drew Carey Show, was molested as a young boy, attempted suicide two times and dropped out of college. It was not until a friend at a radio show asked Drew to write some jokes for his program that Drew began his road to stardom starting with an appearance on Star Search and then Johnny Carson.

In all these cases of Super Achievers failing before they attained greatness, they shared one common factor....FAILURE WAS NOT AN OPTION. You must share this common factor of your desire to become a Super Achiever.

One of the greatest stories of failure, then attaining greatness has rarely been told more convincingly than in the life of one of the most powerful and successful men in the history of America.

1) Failed in first business venture	Age 22
2) Ran for Legislature–DEFEATED	Age 23
3) Failed in second business	Age 24
4) Had a nervous breakdown	Age 27
5) Ran for Speaker in Gov't–DEFEATED	Age 29
6) Ran for Elector in Gov't–DEFEATED	Age 31
7) Ran for Congress–DEFEATED	Age 34
8) Ran for Congress 2nd Time–DEFEATED	Age 39
9) Ran for Senate–DEFEATED	Age 46
10) Ran for Vice President–DEFEATED	Age 47
11) Ran for Senate 2nd Time–DEFEATED	Age 49
12) Ran for President–SUCCESSFUL	Age 51

Who was this great American who, for all intents and purposes should have been considered a failure until he was 51 years old? That would be Abraham Lincoln, one of the greatest Americans of all time and responsible for ending slavery. Now, let me ask you, if failure in life is defined by the number of times you fail, Abraham Lincoln would be considered as one of the greatest failures in governmental history, yet he became known as one of the greatest Presidents of our time. You see, each time Abraham Lincoln failed, he kept using his lessons he learned in failure and applied them to the next goal or challenge in his life until he won the ultimate prize as President of the United States. Attaining Super Achiever status happens at different times in life for different people. That's why you can never let failure stop you from surging ahead, through all setbacks and failures, since you never know when you will finally attain your heart's desires.

These are just some examples of hugely successful people who have failed terribly and experienced tremendous setbacks in their lives yet still, because of their passion, attitude and confidence in themselves, managed to fight through their adversity and become Super Achievers in their lives. Failure is not always a bad thing if you can learn from your mistakes and use the lessons for good.

Remember, Super Achievers succeed in life not because they avoid failure, but because they ARE NOT AFRAID OF FAILURE! DON'T BE AFRAID TO FAIL! IT'S OK.

According to former Coke CEO, Don Keough, there are ten ways to be sure to OBTAIN FAILURE FAST.....AVOID THEM ALL. They are:

1) Stop taking risks. AVOID IT
2) Be content. AVOID IT
3) Before you make any move, take a risk or make a change, ask yourself, "What if I fail". AVOID IT
4) Avoid change. AVOID IT
5) Be inflexible. AVOID IT
6) Be more concerned with your status than service. AVOID IT
7) Avoid focusing on family, friends and loved ones. AVOID IT
8) Put yourself first in all you do. AVOID IT
9) Memorize and live by the phrase, "That's good enough." AVOID IT
10) Accept and rationalize slow growth, productivity and prosperity. AVOID IT.

CHAPTER #4

Creating Luck

CHAPTER 4: Creating Luck

You have said the phrase hundreds of times in your life about yourself or some other individual. "I was lucky" or he or she was lucky. "I was lucky to have gotten that job." "He was lucky to have made the team." What is luck anyway? And does luck truly play a realistic role in peoples lives when they succeed?

First let's understand what luck is. Luck is trying to explain events, outcomes or successes that people do not understand. When there is no clear reason, in the eyes of an individual, why somebody they know got the job or made the team, the answer is always...."It was luck." Was it really luck?

You need to know that although millions of individuals attribute success, achievement, prosperity and wealth to luck, the truth of the matter is THERE ARE NO ACCIDENTS IN LIFE. Success, achievement, prosperity and wealth don't just happen, they are the outcomes of a principle called CAUSE AND EFFECT. This principle is then the cause of another powerful principle called LIFE MOMENTUM. Let me explain.

The law of Cause and Effects Says:

1) A CAUSE: Something you do that causes an effect. (Example: When you......)

2) An Effect: The result of the Cause or the power to produce some result. (Example: You.....)

   a. **When you.......** improve your resume and send it to the employer. (CAUSE), **You.......** Increase your chances of attaining that new job. (EFFECT).

Here are some additional CAUSES and their EFFECTS to help you understand this principle better.

Cause-When You…..	Effect-You…….
1) Increase your contacts	1) Attract people who get you what you want
2) Develop organized work habits	2) Get More & More Things Accomplished
3) Improve prospecting	3) Create more business opportunities
4) Improve networking skills	4) Increase # of people who can impact life.
5) Set goals	5) Develop inner drive & motivation to attain
6) Send extra sales brochures	6) Increase chances of right people seeing it.
7) Read more	7) Increase knowledge and intelligence
8) Take part in trade & industry functions	8) Increase exposure and opportunities
9) Develop strong positive thinking skills	9) You attract into your life positive people
10) When you buy a lotto ticket	10) You increase your chances of winning millions

Once you create the cause, which in turn creates the effect, you have created LIFE MOMENTUM. Life Momentum is continually taking small steps (Causes) towards the achievement of your goals and desires and developing the answers and solutions (Effects) required to achieve them. That's why the harder you work at making progress, the more and better results (LUCK) you will receive.

Take those individuals that have won millions in Lotto. Most people, those who did not even bother to buy a ticket, would say that the winners were just lucky. Were they? They went out and took the time to buy the lotto ticket (CAUSE) and in turn, won the jackpot (EFFECT). Luck? No, just the principle of Cause and Effect. "You've got to be in it to win it" they say!

A phrase said by a gentleman by the name of George Bernard Shaw sums up the principle of Cause and Effect. "The people who get on in this world are the people who get up and look for circumstances they want."

CHAPTER #5

Networking-The People Principle

CHAPTER 5: Networking-The People Principle

This chapter is one of the most important in the entire book. I can not stress enough how critical it is for you to incorporate this chapter's information into your lives as fast as possible if you truly want to attain Super Achiever status in your life.

The phrase, "It's not what you know but who you know", is without question one of the significant phrases in life. Life is all about PEOPLE. Without other PEOPLE impacting your life, supporting you, helping you, advising you, critiquing you, guiding you, referring you and watching out for you, you will never attain your heart' desires. The more people you can develop relationships and friendships with in your towns, schools, jobs, industries etc, the greater your chances of attaining whatever it is in life you so desire. It's called building a NETWORK OF PEOPLE, around you in all areas of your life. People who you can rely on, trust, get along with at all times.

There are two key LAWS you must learn and understand regarding the People Principle.

1) **THE LAW OF RECIPROCITY**: This is one of the most important laws of success. This law says that if you do something nice for someone else, in any way that helps the individual, you create in them an unconscious obligation to pay you back in some way. That's why it is so important to NOT ALWAYS BE CAUGHT UP IN YOURSELF AND YOUR OWN LIFE'S AFFAIRS. Each day, look to see how you can help someone at school, work or at home. If you do this each day, or at least each week, you will be amazed at all the extended hands of help and support you will get in return. The more you give of yourself, the more you get in return.

You will make more friends and partners in two months by becoming interested in and helping in the affairs of other people than you will in two years trying to get people interested in you. Again, this is an amazing principle THAT WORKS. Apply it to your life now!

2) **THE LAW OF LAUGHTER**: This is simple. MAKE PEOPLE LAUGH AND SMILE! People love to laugh and be happy and all people like to be associated with other happy and enjoyable people. The more you make people smile and laugh, the more they are going to want to be around you.

Now, I am not suggesting that you become silly to the extent that you annoy people. Just do your best to always make people smile and occasionally laugh. It will come back to you in immeasurable ways.

CHAPTER #6

Always Remember

CHAPTER 6: Always Remember

I would like to leave you with seven thoughts that I hope you will embrace and incorporate into your life each and every day. They will all inspire you, motivate you and significantly improve the overall quality of your life. They are:

1) You have never lived a perfect day, even though you have earned your money, unless you have done something for someone who will never be able to repay you....Ruth Smeltzer.

2) All good is gained by those whose thought and life are kept pointed close to one main thing, not scattered abroad upon a thousand....Stephen MacKenna.

3) While the Golden Rule is "Treat people as you would like to be treated, The Platinum Rule is to "Treat people as they would like to be treated."

4) Giving of yourself & helping others is the fastest way to success.

5) Universal Law....When you give, you automatically receive.

6) Watch your thoughts; they become words, Watch your words; they become actions, Watch your actions; they become habits, Watch your habits; they become character, Watch your character; it becomes your destiny.

7) Be more concerned with your character than your reputation, because your character is what you really are, while your reputation is merely what others think you are.

I am so excited for you! Why you ask? Because I firmly believe that having finished this book, you have now positioned yourself to attain and achieve goals, desires and dreams in your life that you would have never possessed had you not read this book. You are now already so far ahead of the average individual in terms of your future potential, just by reading this book, that I am 100% confident that you will become a Super Achiever in whatever it is you decide to do or whatever path you decide to take in life.

It has been my honor to have you read my book and I only hope that you embrace the lessons that I have taught you, immediately incorporate them into your life, and take action now on planting the seeds of achievement that will mature and develop you into the human version of the powerful Redwood tree.

Best of luck on your journey to success, prosperity and happiness and remember, you can be or do anything you dream of, as long as you truly believe you can.

www.ingramcontent.com/pod-product-compliance
Lightning Source LLC
La Vergne TN
LVHW091203080426
835509LV00006B/814